A Radical Love

Wisdom from Dorothy Day

Patricia Mitchell, Editor

The Word Among Us Press
9639 Doctor Perry Road
Ijamsville, Maryland 21754
ISBN: 0-932085-45-8

www.wau.org

Cover design by David Crosson

Made and printed in the United States of America

Library of Congress Cataloging-in-Publication Data

Day, Dorothy, 1897-1980.
  A radical love, wisdom from Dorothy Day / Patricia Mitchell, editor.
        p. cm.
  ISBN 0-932085-45-8
          1. Meditations. I Mitchell, Patricia, 1953-II. Title.

BX2182.2 .D365 2000
242—dc21

Table of Contents

Introduction

Dorothy Day always considered herself a radical. Unable to ignore the injustices she saw around her, she championed causes that were intended to protect the less fortunate. After her conversion, however, Day's radical beliefs were grounded not in any political or economic system but in Jesus Christ. When Jesus said to love one another, she believed him—literally.

To Dorothy Day, love meant taking responsibility for her brothers and sisters in Christ. It meant feeding them, clothing them, and standing up for their rights. It meant embracing the poor by living in poverty herself. No wonder one of her favorite quotes was from Fr. Zossima in Dostoyevsky's *The Brothers Karamazov:* "Love in action is a harsh and dreadful thing compared with love in dreams."

For this very reason, Dorothy Day may one day be canonized. When the late Cardinal John O'Connor announced in March 2000 that the opening of her cause for canonization had been approved by the Holy See, he said of her: "Like so many saints of days gone by, she was an idealist in a non-ideal world." It is easy to lose patience with idealists, if only because their standards seem so impossibly high to meet. Dorothy Day well knew that she and Peter Maurin, her cofounder in the Catholic Worker movement, had issued a challenging call to Catholics. She herself was the first to admit her own failure in living up to that call.

Obedience to the Lord. And yet, her vision remains compelling. Day was uncompromising in her obedience to the Lord's call for her life. She saw the needs around her, articulated them, aroused the Catholic conscience to respond to those needs, and strived— whatever the cost—to live the life she was calling others to lead. Many of her ideas anticipated by decades the teachings on social justice of the Second Vatican Council and the call to the laity to participate in the work of the church. As Cardinal O'Connor said, "It was her contention that men and women should begin to live on earth the life they would one day lead in heaven, a life of peace and harmony."

A Radical Love: Wisdom from Dorothy Day is an attempt to capture this vision, a vision founded on the gospel of Christ. Although Dorothy Day lived in very different times—the Worker movement was launched during the Great Depression—her message is timeless. Religion is not intended only for our own personal comfort and solace. As Day herself said, it must go beyond "a matter of Sunday praying" and have vitality. Living the gospel reality that we are all members of the Body of Christ means caring for one another as if we were caring for Christ himself. Christians are called not only to love one another individually but also to change the structures in society that exploit the vulnerable. This is the reality Dorothy Day grasped so well, and which she urged us to live out, precisely because we dare to call ourselves Christians.

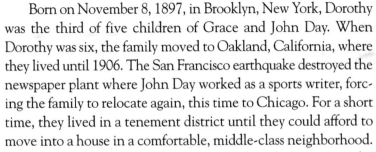

Born on November 8, 1897, in Brooklyn, New York, Dorothy was the third of five children of Grace and John Day. When Dorothy was six, the family moved to Oakland, California, where they lived until 1906. The San Francisco earthquake destroyed the newspaper plant where John Day worked as a sports writer, forcing the family to relocate again, this time to Chicago. For a short time, they lived in a tenement district until they could afford to move into a house in a comfortable, middle-class neighborhood.

Even as a child, Dorothy was sensitive to the inequities she saw around her. She loved to read, and since her father banned dime-store novels and comic books, she read the classics. Upton Sinclair's *The Jungle* so affected her that she took long walks from her own neighborhood to the poor areas Sinclair had described. Her family was not religious and did not attend church. Still, she was deeply affected by the thought of God. "Each time I heard our Lord spoken of," she wrote later about her childhood years, "a warm feeling of joy filled me. It was hearing of someone you love and who loves you." For a time, she attended an Episcopal church with her sister, and developed a love for the Psalms and for the liturgy that remained with her for the rest of her life.

A Hardened Heart. In 1914, at the age of sixteen, Dorothy won a scholarship to the University of Illinois at Urbana, where she became a socialist and rejected organized religion: "I felt at the time that religion would only impede my work. I wanted to have nothing to do with the religion of those whom I saw all about me. I felt that I must turn from it as from a drug. I felt it indeed to be an opiate of the people, so I hardened my heart." When her family moved back to New York two years later, she left the university and found a reporting job for a socialist newspaper in the city.

Over the next few years, Day worked on several labor newspapers and spent her free time with a group of radical writers and intellectuals in Greenwich Village. She lived a bohemian lifestyle and fell desperately in love with an ex-newspaperman. When she became pregnant with his child, she feared that he would abandon her if she did not have an abortion. She went ahead with the abortion—which she did not want—but her lover deserted her anyway. Dorothy was distraught. Several months later, on the rebound, she married an older man, but the union lasted less than a year. After reporting jobs in Chicago and New

Orleans, she returned to New York in 1924. With money she had earned by selling the screen rights to her autobiographical novel, *The Eleventh Virgin*, she purchased a bungalow on the beach in Staten Island.

Surprised by Prayer. In New York she met Forster Batterham, an English biologist who was an anarchist and atheist. After entering into a common-law marriage with him, Day became pregnant. She was overjoyed, and her joy led her, to her own surprise, to pray in thanksgiving. Soon she was attending Sunday Mass and decided her baby would be baptized Catholic. Forster had no use for religion, and Dorothy's new interest in the church created tension between them. When their daughter, Tamar Teresa, was born in March 1926, Dorothy had her baptized. She hesitated in taking that final step herself, knowing that her relationship with Batterham would end. She loved him deeply, and "it was killing me to think of leaving him." Finally, in December of 1927, she made the agonizing decision to sever her union with Forster and was baptized into the Catholic Church.

For the next few years, as a single mother, Dorothy supported herself and Tamar by writing. In December 1932, she went to Washington, D. C. to write an article about a hunger march organized by communists seeking better working conditions for the poor. A great divide now separated her from her former communist and socialist friends, who did not share her faith. Yet Dorothy knew that Catholics should be fighting for the poor, just as the communists were doing. Before leaving Washington, she went to the National Shrine of the Immaculate Conception and offered up "a prayer which came with tears and with anguish, that some way would open up for me to use what talents I possessed for my fellow workers, the poor." When she arrived back in New

York, she found a poorly dressed French immigrant waiting to meet her.

A New Social Order. Peter Maurin was a Catholic laborer and intellectual who sought out Day because he had read her articles. He believed that she was the woman who could help him build a new social order, one founded on Jesus' command to love one another. His revolutionary plan called for "indoctrination"—his word for educating Catholics about the church's social teachings—and he wanted to start a newspaper as well as to sponsor "roundtable discussions" to air these ideas. His program of action included houses of hospitality, where the poor and destitute could find food and shelter, and a life of voluntary poverty—everyone taking less so that others could have more. He emphasized the dignity of the worker and of work itself, and believed this dignity could be more fully realized when people worked the land rather than in mind-numbing factories.

With fifty-seven dollars Dorothy managed to cobble together, the two published the first issue of *The Catholic Worker* in May 1933. The twenty-five hundred copies were sold on the streets for a penny each. The paper was an immediate success with Catholics who were suffering through the Great Depression, and by 1936, circulation had soared to 150,000. At the same time, bread lines formed outside the New York Catholic Worker "house of hospitality." Volunteers from around the country came to staff the house, to care for the poor who lived there, and to become part of the Worker community. Similar Worker houses were formed in other cities. By 1941, thirty-one houses were operating, along with several farming communes.

The Daily Struggle. Despite the success of the movement, life was a struggle. Dorothy found it especially difficult to raise her young daughter amid the squalor and noise of the busy Worker house. Her strength came from her intense prayer life. Day was nourished by a love of Scripture, by daily Mass, and by the lives of the saints. Her favorite saint, Thérèse of Lisieux, reminded her that in the smallest acts of love she performed each day, she was following that "little way" described by the Little Flower. Catholic Worker-sponsored retreats provided her with a renewed sense of vision and refreshment. Even as she criticized the church for failing to live up to its social responsibilities, she continually upheld its doctrinal teachings.

Dorothy Day was a controversial figure. Her unyielding pacifism, even during World War II, brought severe criticism. By the end of the war, only eleven Worker houses remained. Still, she was convinced that her position on nonviolence was based on Jesus' command to love even our enemies. Day traveled around the country giving speeches, supporting worker strikes, and writing firsthand about the poverty and hopelessness that littered the land, even amidst prosperity. The movement survived the war, and the number of Worker houses again began to grow. Today there are 175 Worker houses, each operating independently of one another but all taking on, in one way or another, the vision of Day and Maurin.

Day continued her protests against injustice well into her later years. She was jailed several times in 1955 for refusing to take part in New York's air raid drills and for the last time in 1973, at the age of seventy-six, for a farm worker protest. She died on November 28, 1980, when she was eighty-three years old, surrounded by her daughter Tamar and her grandchildren.

Final Victory. In the end, Dorothy Day would have judged her movement a failure—at least in the sense that it failed to build the new social order that Peter Maurin had envisioned. "Such failure, for those of us who have dedicated our lives to this work, is our cross," she wrote in *The Catholic Worker* in January 1954. Ultimately, she said, the most important thing was to love. Day was a radical. She loved as Jesus loves—in the most radical of ways, by laying her life down for her brothers and sisters. And in that sense, she was victorious.

Dorothy Day was a gifted writer. She was hard-hitting, direct, and did not shy away from describing the more depressing aspects of living the life she had chosen. Whatever her subject, however, she was able to keep God in the picture. There is never any question that the Lord is at the foundation of Day's thoughts and work. Her synthesis of the spiritual and the material—of linking the two into one whole—is evident in all her writing. Her columns are filled with descriptions of the most common events—the warmth of the neighborhood parish, the smells of the kitchen, the sight of men lined up early each morning for bread and coffee. Yet she infuses even these mundane scenes with the glory of God. Quoting St. Catherine of Siena, Day liked to say, "All the way to heaven is heaven." She had the faith to see Christ in the homeless man on the stoop.

Many of the selections in this book were taken from columns Day wrote for *The Catholic Worker* between 1933 and 1980. Day also wrote several books: From *Union Square to Rome* (1938), which she addressed to her communist brother to explain why she had become Catholic; *House of Hospitality* (1939), which described life at the Catholic Worker; her famous autobiography *The Long Loneliness* (1952); *Thérèse* (1960), a biographical essay on St. Thérèse of Lisieux; *Loaves and Fishes* (1963), the story of the origins of the Catholic Worker movement; and *On Pilgrimage* (1948), a book she addressed to women.

Loving Our Neighbor. From this large volume of material, we have tried to find passages that most reflect Day's spirituality and that transcend the specific events of her time to reflect eternal truths. Many will find Day's political stances controversial and challenging, but her reasons for taking those positions were always based on the demands of the gospel. We might see different solutions to the problems she so eloquently described, but that hard question—How do we love our neighbor?—remains ever with us, simply because we are disciples of Christ.

For more information on Dorothy Day, Peter Maurin, or the Catholic Worker movement, there is an informative web site that contains nearly all of Dorothy Day's columns and even some of her books. The Word Among Us would like to give special thanks to those who have designed and maintained that site, since many of the passages in this book were taken from it. *The Dorothy Day Library on the Web* can be accessed at www.catholicworker.org. Day's autobiography, *The Long Loneliness* (Harper San Francisco, 1997), is available in most bookstores.

Perhaps one of the best measures of sainthood is the legacy that a person leaves behind. Twenty years after her death, Dorothy Day is still convicting Christians of their moral obligation to one another. She wanted a "new heaven and a new earth wherein justice dwelleth." Though we will certainly fail in countless ways, let us take up the work that the Lord has given to us to build heaven on earth.

Patricia Mitchell
Editor

No Gingerbread Saint

The late Cardinal John O'Connor of New York believed that Dorothy Day was a saint, "not a 'gingerbread' saint or a 'holy card' saint, but a modern-day devoted daughter of the church." In November 1997, on the centenary of her birth, he proposed initiating Day's canonization process. On March 16, 2000, the cardinal announced that the Holy See had approved the archdiocese's petition to open the Cause for Beatification and Canonization of Dorothy Day and had given her the title "Servant of God." The following are excerpts taken from O'Connor's homily at Sunday Mass in St. Patrick's Cathedral in New York City on November 9, 1997:

She had died before I became Archbishop of New York, or I would have called on her immediately upon my arrival. Few people have had such an impact on my life, even though we never met.

Dorothy Day was born on November 8, 1897, and died November 29, 1980. Hardly a seminarian of my era escaped her influence. Rare was the young priest untouched by her life. Whether or not we honored in our own lives her passionate commitment to the poor, or followed even distantly in her footsteps, she *worried* us. That was her gift to us, a gift I still cherish as I try to maneuver my own perilous way among the accoutrements and "practicalities" of life as a Cardinal Archbishop of New York. . . .

Before knowing of Dorothy Day I worried about poverty (in kind of an effete way); since then, I worry about poor people. Homelessness doesn't bother me any more, or hunger (these are abstractions that we can talk about in works on sociology, in big tomes on economics and political speeches); homeless and hungry people worry the life out of me. . . .

I wish every woman who has ever suffered an abortion (including perhaps someone or several in this church) would come to know Dorothy Day. Her story was so typical. Made pregnant by a man who insisted she have an abortion, who then abandoned her anyway, she suffered terribly for what she had done, and later pleaded with others not to do the same. But later, too, after becoming a Catholic, she learned the love and mercy of the Lord, and knew she never had to worry about His forgiveness. . . .

Radical though she was, her respect for and commitment and obedience to Church teaching were unswerving. Indeed, those of us who grew up knowing her recognized early in the game that she was a radical precisely because she was a believer, a believer and a practitioner. She, in fact, chided those who wanted to join her in her works of social justice, but who, in her judgment, didn't take the Church seriously enough, and didn't bother about getting to Mass. . . .

So where do we go from here? Do we celebrate this 100th anniversary and go home and think, "Wasn't that nice that Dorothy Day did all those things?" Since Dorothy Day lived and worked and died here in New York, I receive many letters urging me, as the Archbishop of New York, to initiate her cause for canonization. I ask myself prayerfully and carefully if I should do so. It seems to me that this would be a wise and prudent course of action. . . .

There are those who believe that because she was a protester against some things that people confuse with Americanism itself that her cause should not be submitted. I disagree completely with that position. Some believe that her cause should not be initiated because of their contempt for Church processes. They believe that the whole concept of formal canonization is "folderol," costing a lot of money and carried out with no holiness. I disagree with that position.

There are some who believe that Dorothy Day was indeed a living saint, that the cause of canonization need not therefore be processed. Perhaps. But why does the Church canonize saints? In part so that their person, their works, their lives will become that much better known and that they will encourage others to follow in their footsteps. And, of course, that the Church may say formally and officially—"This is sanctity, this is the road to eternal life, to feed the hungry, to clothe the naked, to house the homeless, to love every human person made in the image and likeness of God." It is this and nothing else: Our Lord summarized it all—"You shall love the Lord your God with your whole heart, your whole soul, your whole mind, your whole strength and your neighbor as yourself."

I wish I had known Dorothy Day personally. I feel that I know her because of her goodness. But surely, if any woman ever loved God and her neighbor it was Dorothy Day! Pray that we do what we should do.

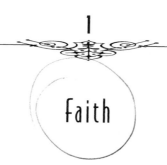

Faith

A LONELY REVOLUTION

We have all probably noted those sudden moments of quiet—those strange and almost miraculous moments in the life of a big city when there is a cessation of traffic noises—just an instant when there is only the sound of footsteps which serves to emphasize a sudden peace. During those seconds it is possible to notice the sunlight, to notice our fellow humans, to take breath.

After hours of excitement and action and many human contacts, when even in one's sleep and at moments of waking there is a sense of the imminence of things to be done and of conflict ahead, it is good to seek those moments of perfect stillness and refreshment during early Mass.

Then indeed it seems that God touches the heart and the mind. There are moments of recollection, of realization when the path seems straighter, the course to be followed perfectly plain, though not easy. It is as though the great Physician to whom we go for healing had put straight that which was dislocated, and prescribed a course of action so definite that we breathe relief at having matters taken out of our hands.

Such a moment came this morning with the thought—the revolution we are engaged in is a lonely revolution, fought out in our own hearts, a struggle between Nature and Grace.

It is the most important work of all in which we are engaged.

If we concentrate our energies primarily on that, then we can trust those impulses of the Holy Spirit and follow them simply, without question. We can trust and believe that all things will work together for good to them that love God, and that He will guide and direct us in our work. We will accomplish just what He wishes us to accomplish and no more, regardless of our striving. Since we have good will, one need no longer worry as though the work depended just on ourselves. ❧

The Catholic Worker
December 1934

ALL THE WAY TO HEAVEN IS HEAVEN

The spring peepers have begun their shrill sweet song each evening as we leave the chapel after rosary. It is still frosty and when the wind comes from the west it is biting, but the flowers are blooming, a mass of gold and purple, a conquering color, life victorious over death. We are beginning to look for dandelions for spring salad, and we wake to the singing of birds again.

Today, the wind is from the south and I can write with my door open so that I can look down over the yellow fields, and into the mass of rose maple and violet which is the color of the woods today. Outside my window the lilac buds are bursting out. Crows cry out in the woods. Starlings confer.

The way to God is surely through the exterior senses on a day like this. The round-bellied little puppy tied up by the back door, that Paul assured us has quite a touch of collie; that delightful Christina Maria who sings and smiles at four months—and my own grandchildren with their dirty hands clutching bouquets of maple blossoms for the chapel all show us the tenderness of God. All the way to heaven is heaven.

The Catholic Worker
April 1954

No Room for Discouragement

There were six of us at Mass this morning and the morning was cool, with a haze coming up from the river. Around on Washington Street, under the New York Central tracks, there is grass growing and there are crickets in that grass. A window box on the fire escape of a tenement is lush with balsam and petunia.

The sun sparkles on the river and the boats plough joyously through the choppy water. These are the things that make thanksgiving easy to continue during the day.

Every good impulse, every noble deed we perform is of God, Christ in us. At the very same time there is an evil, complacent nagging going on, trying to discourage us, trying to impugn our motives, trying to spoil everything of good we do. This complacency, self-satisfaction, is to be scorned and silenced. It shows pride even to be surprised and grieved at the baseness, like sediment, at the bottom of every good deed. As long as we live there will be a war, a conflict between nature and grace, nature again and again getting the upper hand for the moment, only to be put down rigidly. If we have faith and hope, it is impossible to be discouraged.

Chapter Six
House of Hospitality

CHRIST IN THE BREAD

St. Teresa says that Christ is disguised as bread so that we will not fear to approach Him—so that we can go to Him in confidence, daily, needing Him daily as we need our physical bread.

We are not, most of us, capable of exalted emotion, save rarely. We are not capable always of feelings of love, awe, gratitude, and repentance. So Christ has taken the form of bread that we may more readily approach Him, and feeding daily, assimilating Christ so that it is not we but Christ working in us, we may be made more capable of understanding and realizing and loving Him.

Yes, in bread Christ has become so simple—has condescended so far, that a child can eat the Sacred Food with love and gratitude. He said that we would be scandalized, so it is no use for me to be surprised and horrified at the bluntness of your objection. Even the nearest and dearest of His friends dispersed and fled, not realizing the mystery of the Redemption, that Christ was laying down His life for all men.

When He prayed in agony in the garden—when the weight of our sins descended upon Him, all the sins that had been and that would be committed throughout the world forever after; when He suffered all the temptations, all the horror, all the remorse for the rest of the world—His disciples did not understand that either. He watched and suffered alone in His agony. He had told them that the next day He was to die. And in spite of His miracles they paid so little attention to His words that they slept, as the Friend they loved most in the world struggled against the thought of His death. They left Him alone, they slept, and the next day they fled, so little did they understand His teachings, though they had been with Him for three years. They did not understand even after they had eaten with Him at the Last Supper. They did not understand until the Holy Spirit descended upon them and it was *given* to them to understand.

Chapter Thirteen
From Union Square to Rome

Only the H.S. can open our eyes!

AN EFFORT OF THE WILL

Tamar Teresa [Day's daughter], this Sunday afternoon, was full of the excitement of counting up her mortifications for Lent. She was beginning well, with zest and enthusiasm. What were her mortifications? Eggs and candy and silence. The first you eat, the second you don't eat (but you are allowed cookies even with icing on them), and the third—well, silent periods one must learn to enjoy because of offering them up. These mortifications were for the convent life in general. During school hours there were sacrifices such as not looking out the window—and that is a tremendous one considering the forty days of Lent and spring on its way, and maple trees budding and starlings calling and two friendly old crows cheering the spring together.

Only yesterday, too, she looked out and soldiers were going down the country road and sacrifices and mortifications were forgotten in the joy of watching the marchers.

But in general, in the first flush of Lent, the struggle is undertaken bravely.

What if during the long weeks the fervor lessens and the work of accumulating graces was continued with many lapses, but by effort of will.

That time when *will* has to be brought into play is perhaps the most important of all, despite failures and the total lack of a sense of accomplishment, of growth.

Fervor comes again with Holy Week, joy comes on the day of resurrection, with all nature singing exultantly God's praises.

To keep united to God through the suffering Humanity of His son—that is the aim of Lent. ༄

The Catholic Worker
April 1935

I AM CONVINCED OF GOD'S LOVE

There is the question, why did Christ institute this Sacrament of His Body and Blood? And the answer is very simple. It was because He loved us and wished to be with us. "My delights are to be with the children of men." He made us and He loves us. His presence in the Blessed Sacrament is the great proof of that love.

St. Teresa of Avila said that we should meditate more on the love of God for us, rather than our love for Him. And she emphasizes His sacred Humanity and says that by never losing sight of that it is easier for us to realize that love. She is always talking about the Man Jesus.

But it is hard to understand the love of God for us. We pray daily to increase in the love of God because we know that if we love a person very much, all things become easy to us and delightful. We want, rather unreasonably, sensible feelings of love. St. Teresa says that the only way we can measure the love we have for God, is the love we have for our fellows. So by working for our fellows we come to love them. That you understand, for you believe that you are working for them when you give hours every morning to the distribution of literature, climbing tenement-house stairs, knocking at doors, suffering rebuffs, enduring heat and cold, weariness and hardships to bring to them what you consider a gospel which will set them free.

And if you and I love our faulty fellow-human beings, how much more must God love us all? If we, as human parents, can forgive our children any neglect, any crime, and work and pray patiently to make them better, how much more does God love us?

You may say perhaps: "How do we know He does, if there is a He!" And I can only answer that we know it because He is here present with us today in the Blessed Sacrament on the altar, that He never has left us, and that by daily going to Him for the gift of Himself as daily bread, I am convinced of that love. I have the Faith that feeding at that table has nourished my soul so that there is life in it, and a lively realization that there is such a thing as the love of Christ for us. ❧

Chapter Thirteen
From Union Square to Rome

FINDING THE WAY

These days I can never look up at the sky and see the moon without thinking with wonder and awe that men have walked there. To conceive of such a thing—to desire such an adventure, to be capable of overcoming all fear, all doubt, to have faith in man's ability to solve problems, and seek out the way to go about this great exploration—what dedication of mind and will! "What is man that thou art mindful of him? Thou hast made him little less than the angels." It keeps coming into my mind—how much man would be capable of if his soul were strong in the love of God, if he wanted God as much as he wanted to penetrate the power and glory of God's creation.

To know Him, to love Him, and to serve Him—a personal God, who took on human flesh and became man and suffered and died for us. To find the way, not to the moon but to God—this is man's real desire, because of his need for love, and God is love.

The Catholic Worker
March-April 1976

2

Poverty

CHRIST CAME FOR THE POOR

I do not know how to love God except by loving the poor. I do not know how to serve God except by serving the poor. Poor people are those people who are standing out in the rain now, today, May 29, standing there with the rain soaking through their thin clothes, running down their faces like tears. They are standing there because they are hungry, and because in our fifteen-foot by fifty-foot dining room and kitchen there is warmth, and there is Everet Trebtoske and his staff, serving soup, a good heavy pea soup, with bread. Poor people are people like that colored man and woman who spent the night riding in the subways because they had been put out of their lodging, after they had lost their jobs and spent what little they had laid by. A priest sent them to us last night. There was no hospice in his parish, no Christ rooms. Poor people is that sick man who has epileptic fits and cannot hold a job and who keeps trying because he doesn't want to go on relief. Poor people is that woman in jail who wants to come to us when she gets out, and that alcoholic dim-witted prostitute who plies her trade on the Bowery. It is that drunkard sleeping in a doorway, that old woman going through garbage cans. Sinners are poor people, only it is getting so that only the poor are considered sinners these days. We are supposed not only to love sinners, but to have reverence for them, Fr. Faber said, because Christ came especially for them. ❧

The Catholic Worker
June 1950

THE MYSTERY OF POVERTY

On Easter Day, on awakening late after the long midnight services in our parish church, I read over the last chapter of the four gospels and felt that I had received great light and understanding with the reading of them. "They have taken the Lord out of His tomb and we do not know where they have laid Him," Mary Magdalene said, and we can say this with her in times of doubt and questioning. How do we know we believe? How do we know we indeed have faith? Because we have seen His hands and His feet in the poor around us. He has shown Himself to us in them. We start by loving them for Him, and we soon love them for themselves, each one a unique person, most special!

In that last glorious chapter of St. Luke, Jesus told His followers, "Why are you so perturbed? Why do questions arise in your minds? Look at My hands and My feet. It is I Myself. Touch Me and see. No ghost has flesh and bones as you can see I have." They were still unconvinced, for it seemed too good to be true. "So He asked them, 'Have you anything to eat?' They offered Him a piece of fish they had cooked which He took and ate before their eyes."

How can I help but think of these things every time I sit down at Chrystie Street or Peter Maurin Farm and look around at the tables filled with the unutterably poor who are going through their long-continuing crucifixion. It is most surely an exercise of faith for us to see Christ in each other. But it is through such exercise that we grow and the joy of our vocation assures us we are on the right path.

Most certainly, it is easier to believe now that the sun warms us, and we know that buds will appear on the sycamore trees in the wasteland across from the Catholic Worker office, that life will spring out of the dull clods of that littered park across the way. There are wars and rumors of war, poverty and plague, hunger and pain. Still, the sap is rising, again there is the resurrection of spring, God's continuing promise to us that He is with us always, with His comfort and joy, if we will only ask.

The mystery of the poor is this: That they are Jesus, and what you do for them you do for Him. It is the only way we have of knowing and believing in our love. The mystery of poverty is that by sharing in it, making ourselves poor in giving to others, we increase our knowledge of and belief in love. ❧

The Catholic Worker
April 1964

WE MUST DO WHAT WE CAN

Poverty is a strange and elusive thing. I have tried to write about it, its joys and its sorrows, for thirty years now; and I could probably write about it for another thirty without conveying what I feel about it as well as I would like. I condemn poverty and I advocate it; poverty is simple and complex at once; it is a social phenomenon and a personal matter. Poverty is an elusive thing, and a paradoxical one.

We need always to be thinking and writing about it, for if we are not among its victims its reality fades from us. We must talk about poverty because people insulated by their own comfort lose sight of it. So many good souls who visit us tell how they were brought up in poverty, but how, through hard work and cooperation, their parents managed to educate all the children—even raise up priests and nuns for the Church. They contend that healthful habits and a stable family situation enable people to escape from the poverty class, no matter how mean the slum they may once have been forced to live in. The argument runs, so why can't everybody do it? No, these people don't know about the poor. Their concept of poverty is of something as neat and well-ordered as a nun's cell. . . .

In front of me as I write is Fritz Eichenberg's picture of St. Vincent de Paul (Fritz, a Quaker, does the woodcuts in *The Catholic Worker*). He holds a chubby child in his arms, and a thin, pale child is clinging to him. Yes, the poor will always be with us—Our Lord told us that—and there will always be a need for our sharing, for stripping ourselves to help others. It is—and always will be—a lifetime job. But I am sure that God did not intend that there be so many poor. The class struggle is of *our* making and by *our* consent, not His, and we must do what we can to change it. ∼

Chapter Six
Loaves and Fishes

THE CALL TO THE LAITY

Our poverty is not a stark and dreary poverty, because we have the security which living together brings. But it is that very living together that is often hard. Beds crowded together, much coming and going, people sleeping on the floor, no bathing facilities, only cold water. These are the hardships. Poverty means lack of paint, it means bedbugs, cockroaches and rats and the constant war against these. Poverty means body lice. A man fainted on the coffee line some months ago and just holding his head to pour some coffee between his drawn lips meant picking up a few bugs. Poverty means lack of soap and Lysol and cleansing powders. (How to provide soap, for instance, for two hundred and fifty men, such as the Pittsburgh house takes care of? Or even of the forty-five or so we have here?)

But how are we going to do the work without poverty? How are we going to reach the unemployed, the organized and unorganized workers, and the destitute, with the teachings of the gospel, the social teachings of the Church? How are we going to have money to pay for printing the paper, to buy bread, sugar, coffee, milk, for a thousand hungry people daily, unless we do without salaries, live together in a donated tenement?

We are using the means always used by the Church in missionary work. It is true that it was generally religious orders which used these means.

But Pope Pius XI called for a lay apostolate. It is the work of our time which every Catholic must be engaged in as much as he can. There is no one who could not make more sacrifices to feed the poor, to clothe the naked. To follow Christ we have got to aim to be poor as He was.

The Catholic Worker
September 1939

THE PEARL OF GREAT PRICE

The reason for our existence is to praise God, to love Him and serve Him, and we can do this only by loving our brothers. "All men are brothers." This is the great truth that makes us realize God. Great crimes, it is true, have been committed in the name of human brotherhood; that may serve to obscure the truth, but we must keep on saying it. We must keep on saying it because Love is the reason for our existence. It is what we all live for, whether we are a hanger-on in Times Square or the most pious member of a community. We are seeking what we think to be the good for us. If we don't know any better, often it is because radio, newspapers, press, and pulpit have neglected so to inform us. We love what is presented to us to love, and God is not much presented. It is as hard to see Jesus in the respectable Christian today as in the man on the Bowery. And so "the masses have been lost to the Church."

We who live in this country cannot be as poor as those who go out to other countries. This is so rich a country that luxury has developed at the expense of necessities, and even the destitute partake of the luxury. We are the rich country of the world, like Dives at the feast. We must try hard, we must study to be poor like Lazarus at the gate, who was taken into Abraham's bosom. The gospel doesn't tell us anything about Lazarus' virtues. He just sat there and let the dogs lick his sores. He would be classed by any social worker of today as a mental case. But again, poverty, and in this case destitution, like hospitality, is so esteemed by God, it is something to be sought after, worked for, the pearl of great price. ❧

The Catholic Worker
July-August 1953

THE HARSH REALITIES

I am convinced that if we had an understanding and a love of poverty we would begin to be as free and joyous as St. Francis, who had a passion for Lady Poverty and lives on with us in joyous poverty through all the centuries since his death.

It is hard to write about poverty. We live in a slum neighborhood that is becoming ever more crowded with Puerto Ricans who are doubling up in unspeakably filthy, dark, crowded tenements on the lower east side and in Harlem, who have the lowest wages in the city, who do the hardest work, who are little and undernourished from generations of privation and exploitation by us. We used to have a hard time getting rid of all the small-sized clothes which came in to us. Ladies who could eat steak and salads and keep their slim figures, contributed good clothes, small-sized shoes, and I can remember Julia Porcelli saying once, "Why are the poor always fat? We never get enough clothes to fit them." The American poor may be fat with the starches they eat, but the Puerto Rican poor are lean. The stock in the clothes room at Chrystie Street moves quickly now.

It is hard to write about poverty when a visitor tells you of how he and his family all lived in a basement room and did sweatshop work at night to make ends meet, and how the landlord came in and belabored them for not paying his exorbitant rent.

It is hard to write about poverty when the backyard at Chrystie Street still has the stock of furniture piled to one side that was put out on the street in an eviction in a next-door tenement. 〰

The Catholic Worker
May 1952

PUTTING OFF THE OLD MAN

The only way we have to show our love for God is by the love we have for our brother. "Inasmuch as you have done it unto one of the least of these My brethren, you have done it unto Me." "You love God as much as the one you love the least."

Love of brother means voluntary poverty, stripping one's self, putting off the old man, denying one's self, etc. It also means non-participation in those comforts and luxuries which have been manufactured by the exploitation of others. While our brothers suffer, we must compassionate them, suffer with them. While our brothers suffer from lack of necessities, we will refuse to enjoy comforts. These resolutions, no matter how hard they are to live up to, no matter how often we fall and have to begin over again, are part of the vision and the long-range view which Peter Maurin has been trying to give us these past ten years. . . . And we must keep this vision in mind, recognize the truth of it, the necessity for it, even though we do not, can not, live up to it. Like perfection. We are ordered to be perfect as our heavenly Father is perfect, and we aim at it, in our intention, though in our execution we may fall short of the mark over and over. St. Paul says, it is by little and by little that we proceed. ⌇

The Catholic Worker
December 1944

Denying Christ in His Poor

I remembered how I spoke down in Palm Beach last month before the Four Arts Club, on the invitation of a convert. They told me, when I had finished, "you know we never pay speakers," and another woman said, with a tremor, "Miss Day, I hope you can convey to your readers and listeners, that we would give our very souls to help the poor, if we saw any constructive way of doing it." And still another told me, "The workers come to my husband's mill and beg him with tears in their eyes to save them from corrupt union leaders. I hope you don't mind my saying so, but I think you are all wrong when it comes to unions."

They all were deeply moved, they told me, at the picture of conditions in Arkansas and the steel districts and the coal mining districts, but, "You can't do anything with them, you know, these poor people. It seems to me the best remedy is birth control and sterilization."

We are told, and we try always to keep a just attitude toward the rich, but as I thought of our breakfast line, our crowded house with people sleeping on the floor, when I thought of cold tenement apartments around us, and the lean gaunt faces of the men who come to us for help, desperation in their eyes, it is impossible not to hate, with a hearty hatred and with a strong anger, the injustices of this world.

St. Thomas says that anger is not a sin, provided there go not with it an undue desire for revenge. We want no revolutions, we want the brotherhood of men. We want men to love one another. We want all men to have sufficient for their needs. But when we meet people who deny Christ in His poor, we feel, "Here are atheists indeed."

At the same time that I put down these melancholy thoughts, I am thinking of Michael Martin, porter, and the hosts of readers and friends the Catholic Worker has who have spread the work far and wide, who not only help us to keep the coffee line going, but who on their own account are performing countless works of mercy. And my heart swells with love and gratitude to the great mass of human beings who are one with their fellows, who love our Lord and try to serve Him and show their love to His poor.

Our pastor said recently that 60 million of our 130 million here in the United States professed no religion, and I thought with grief that it was the fault of those professing Christians who repelled the others. They turned first from Christ crucified because He was a poor worker, buffeted and spat upon and beaten. And now—strange thought—the devil has so maneuvered it that the people turn from Him because those who profess Him are clothed in soft raiment and sit at well spread tables and deny the poor. ❧

The Catholic Worker
April 1937

CHOSEN BY CHRIST

Every one of us who was attracted to the poor had a sense of guilt, of responsibility, a feeling that in some way we were living on the labor of others. The fact that we were born in a certain environment, were enabled to go to school, were endowed with the ability to compete with others and hold our own, that we had few physical disabilities—all these things marked us as the privileged in a way. We felt a respect for the poor and destitute as those nearest to God, as those chosen by Christ for His compassion. Christ lived among men. The great mystery of the Incarnation, which meant that God became man that man might become God, was a joy that made us want to kiss the earth in worship, because His feet once trod that same earth. ✐

Part Three
The Long Loneliness

EMBRACING POVERTY

We in our generation have more and more come to consider the state as bountiful Uncle Sam. "Uncle Sam will take care of it all. The race question, the labor question, the unemployment question." We will all be registered and tabulated and employed or put on a dole, and shunted from clinic to birth control clinic. "What right have people who have no work to have a baby?" How many poor Catholic mothers heard that during those grim years before the war! . . .

But who is to take care of them if the government does not? That is a question in a day when all are turning to the state, and when people are asking, "Am I my brother's keeper?" Certainly we all should know that it is not the province of the government to practice the works of mercy, or go in for insurance. Smaller bodies, decentralized groups, should be caring for all such needs.

The first unit of society is the family. The family should look after its own and, in addition, as the early fathers said, "Every home should have a Christ room in it, so that hospitality may be practiced." "The coat that hangs in your closet belongs to the poor." "If your brother is hungry, it is your responsibility."

"When did we see Thee hungry, when did we see Thee naked?" People either plead ignorance or they say, "It is none of my responsibility." But we are all members one of another, so we are obliged in conscience to help each other. The parish is the next unit, and there are local councils of the St. Vincent de Paul Society. Then there is the city, and the larger body of charitable groups. And there are the unions, where mutual aid and fraternal charity is also practiced. For those who are not Catholics, there are lodges and fraternal organizations, where there is a long tradition of charity. But now there is a dependence on the state. Hospitals once Catholic are subsidized by the state. Orphanages once supported by Catholic charity receive their aid from community chests. And when it is not the state it is bingo parties!

The poor mother of six cannot reject the one hundred and eighty dollars. She cannot say, "Keep your miserable, puny, insufficient one hundred and eighty dollars which you give me in exchange for my husband." She has poverty, Involuntary poverty.

But we must reject it. We must keep on talking about voluntary poverty, and holy poverty, because it is only if we can consent to strip ourselves that we can put on Christ. It is only if we love poverty that we are going to have the means to help others. If we love poverty we will be free to give up a job, to speak when we feel it would be wrong to be silent. We can only talk about voluntary poverty because we believe Christians must be fools for Christ. We can only embrace voluntary poverty in the light of faith. ❧

The Catholic Worker
February 1945

LUXURY EVEN IN JAIL

When you go to jail you finally feel that you are being stripped of whatever you have. You look on as the police empty your handbag. You start right out being humiliated by having so much in your handbag. I remember when we first demonstrated against taking shelter in an air-raid drill, in 1955. There were twenty-eight of us and we had to be photographed, fingerprinted, stripped, showered, and examined. It went on until four in the morning. We were put in tiny cells that were anything but clean; the mattresses were stained and dirty. You look at the equipment of a city prison in the great city of New York in the richest country of the world and you think how unbelievable it is that they cannot afford anything better than this for their prisoners.

There's a little element of fear there too because one of the things that has been done when people are in prison for conscience is to instigate, to build up resentment, especially in wartime, among the other prisoners, by saying that pacifists are spies, communists, etc.; people have been maltreated and abused in prison because of this. There is also the hostility between Negroes and whites that is quite apt to break out, so that there is an element of fear in your imagination that conjures up these things.

But in general, there is a feeling of relief when you are in prison. Here you are now, stripped of everything, no responsibility of any kind, no telephones, no mail; you are there, and Holy Mother the State is taking care of you. The food in the city prison was good, just as good as Catholic Worker food, and there was a great abundance of it. As a matter of fact, we saw so much being thrown out after every meal, as it is in the army, and thought, what a horrible waste.

The cells were small, we were confined and got little air; there were tiny little windows and we almost stifled in summertime. So we had our discomforts. But there was a commissary and I was able to buy some instant coffee and take my missal and lie down on my cot free of all responsibility. So there was luxury even there. ∾

The Catholic Worker
April 1968

3

Prayer

UNITED IN PRAISE

The two great commandments are to love God and to love our brothers. When we are praying the official prayers of the Church, uniting in praise, we are loving God. And because we are praying together, we are loving each other. Some may say this doesn't follow. Margaret may have just had an argument with John about money for carrots; Joe Smolko may have just accused Texas of getting out of washing the dishes; John Cort and Bill Callahan may have been combating each other over what is a just war. But just the same, we know that when we are united together in the community room in this evening prayer, we are conscious of a Christian solidarity. As members of the Church, we are united to the whole Church. We are united with Christ Himself who is head of the Mystical Body. We may not do it very well, our poor efforts may be feeble, our hearts may not be right, but the will is there, and united with

Him we partake of His merits. He is the only one who can pray right, and we are praying with Him so our prayer is effective. Then too, we are united with each other, and we benefit by all the merits and graces of our brethren. We lift each other up. "Two are better than one, for if one falls the other lifts him up." "A brother who is helped by his brother is like a strong city." ∾

Chapter Twelve
House of Hospitality

THE AFTER EFFECTS OF PRAYER

Two of the girls in the House of Hospitality have been fighting constantly. Today I felt so bad about it I could have wept. I am so enraged that anyone should so consistently, month after month, act in mean, little, underhanded ways that I almost wanted to beat them both. My mind was in a turmoil and yet I could not stop it. I went to church leaving word for Tina to meet me there and she came and stayed until after the rosary. (She must be getting to feel quite at home in church.) Afterwards, we went to the movies and saw a really delightfully funny film with Butterworth in it, and then we went home, both of us with raging headaches. It had been very hot all day. At the house, it was still noisy and I wept before going to sleep, and awoke with the same feeling of oppression. To Mass and Communion, still feeling oppressed, praying with distraction. And yet it rather amused me too to place the two girls together in the hands of our Blessed Mother. But it worked!

Despite my feeling of almost hopelessness and desperation, humanly speaking, I came through the day feeling singularly calm, peaceful, and happy.

Three conclusions were the result of my praying: First: My getting into a temper helped nobody. But remaining loving towards all helped to calm them all. Hence a great responsibility rests on me. Second: It was cruel to be harsh to anyone so absolutely dependent, as they are, humanly, on my kindness. Third: It is a healthy sign that they are not crushed and humbled toward other human beings by their own miseries. I mean, going around meekly for fear of me, or being humble out of human respect. . . .

Let reform come through love of God only, and from that love of God, love of each other.

The epistle or gospel, I forget which, for St. Paulinus' day is especially beautiful: "Out of your abundance supply their want." Which means charity and patience and love, as well as material goods, and abilities to help actively in the movement. It has been doing me good all week.

This morning it was the Offertory of the Sacred Heart Mass which caught my eye. Why should we expect consolations? It is good and healthy to be oppressed, a great opportunity for growth. We are driven to prayer, we are loath and comfortless. But as Dom Chapman says, "It is the after effects which count."

And the after effects of last night's and this morning's heavy praying have been peace and joy and strength and thanksgiving and a great deal of humility too, at being so weak that God had to send me consolation to prepare me for the next trial.

I should know by this time that just because I *feel* that everything is useless and going to pieces and badly done and futile, it is not really that way at all. Everything is all right. It is in the hands of God. Let us abandon everything to Divine Providence.

And I must remember too that often beautiful scenery or a perfect symphony leaves me cold and dreary. There is nothing the matter either with the scenery or the music—it is myself. I have endured other miseries cheerfully at times. So I must be calm, patient, enduring, and meditate on the gifts of the Holy Spirit.

I am writing this for my consolation and courage some future day when God sees fit and thinks me strong enough to bear longer-continued crosses.

It is to remind myself so that maybe I will be stronger.

Chapter Six
House of Hospitality

ASKING FOR WHAT WE NEED

W e've been reading the Old Testament a great deal this summer; and when we pray importunately for these material needs, because we have a very large and hungry family of about a hundred, we are reminded of the words of Moses. When Pharaoh, tired of the disasters which were overtaking him, and yet greedy, told Moses to take his people and get out, only leaving the herds behind him, Moses refused. "There shall not a hoof remain of them," he said, "for they are necessary for the service of the Lord Our God."

And I do indeed feel that all these things I have been mentioning "are necessary for the service of the Lord Our God," so we shall continue to pray for them. ∾

Chapter Twelve
House of Hospitality

LIVING THE LITURGICAL DAY

T he basis of the liturgical movement is prayer, the liturgical prayer of the church. It is a revolt against private, individual prayer. St. Paul said, "We know not what we should pray for as we ought, but the Spirit Himself asketh for us with unspeakable groanings." When we pray thus we pray *with* Christ, not *to* Christ. When we recite prime and compline we are using the inspired prayer of the church. When we pray *with* Christ (not *to* Him) we realize Christ as our Brother. We think of all men as our brothers then, as members of the Mystical Body of Christ. "We are all members, one of another," and, remembering this, we can never be indifferent to the social miseries and evils of the day. The dogma of the Mystical Body has tremendous social implications. . . .

Once we heard a woman at a Catholic Action convention say, "Are you going to the liturgical lecture?" and her friend replied, "I am not interested in music." Many people confuse liturgy with rubric—with externals. . . .

Living the liturgical day as much as we are able, beginning with prime, using the missal, ending the day with compline and so going through the liturgical year we find that it is now not us, but Christ in us, who is working to combat injustice and oppression. We are on our way to becoming "other Christs."

We cannot build up the idea of the apostolate of the laity without the foundation of the liturgy.

The Catholic Worker
January 1936

GOD TAKES OVER

A few years ago an old woman died in our midst, here at our House of Hospitality in New York. She was surrounded by many men and women she had known a long time; she had the best of care. We had a nurse living with us who could meet any emergency. But Catherine, the last few weeks of her life, often clutched at my hand as I passed her, and would plead with me, "There is a God, tell me there is a God! Tell me!"

I could only say, "Yes, Catherine, there is a God. He is our Father and He loves us, you and me." When you say these things it is an act of faith. You feel your helplessness so you pray harder. You seem to know nothing, you can only hold her hand and make your affirmation. So much of our prayer is made up of these affirmations. "I praise Thee, O God, I bless Thee. What have I on earth but Thee and what do I desire in heaven besides Thee?" I am saying this *for* Catherine, *instead* of Catherine, because she is in "the valley of the shadow."

But did I comfort her? A few days later a young girl said to me, "The word Father means nothing to me. It brings me no comfort. I had a drunken father who abused my mother and beat his children." We can do nothing by our words. So we are driven to prayer by our helplessness. God takes over. ❧

The Catholic Worker
March-April 1976

LIFE SHOT THROUGH WITH GLORY

It was in Chicago, where we moved to afterward, that I met my first Catholic. It was the first time we had been really poor. We lived in an apartment over a store, on Cottage Grove Avenue. There was no upstairs, no garden, no sense of space. The tenement stretched way down the block and there were back porches and paved courtyards with never a touch of green anywhere. I remember how hungry I became for the green fields during the long hot summer that followed. There was a vacant lot over by the lake front and I used to walk down there with my sister and stand sniffing ecstatically the hot sweet smell of wild clover and listening to the sleepy sound of the crickets. But that very desire for beauty was a painful delight for me. It sharpened my senses and made me more avid in my search for it. I found it in the lake that stretched steel gray beyond the Illinois Central tracks. I found it in that one lone field of clover. And I found a glimpse of supernatural beauty in Mrs. Barrett, mother of Kathryn and six other little Barretts, who lived upstairs.

It was Mrs. Barrett who gave me my first impulse towards Catholicism. It was around ten o'clock in the morning that I went up to Kathryn's to call for her to come out and play. There was no one on the porch or in the kitchen. The breakfast dishes had all been washed. They were long railroad apartments, those flats, and thinking the children must be in the front room, I burst in and ran through the bedrooms.

In the front bedroom Mrs. Barrett was on her knees, saying her prayers. She turned to tell me that Kathryn and the children had all gone to the store and went on with her praying. And I felt a warm burst of love toward Mrs. Barrett that I have never forgotten, a feeling of gratitude and happiness that still warms my heart when I remember her. She had God, and there was beauty and joy in her life.

All through my life what she was doing remained with me. And though I became oppressed with the problem of poverty and injustice, though I groaned at the hideous sordidness of man's lot, though there were years when I clung to the philosophy of economic determinism as an explanation of man's fate, still there were moments when in the midst of misery and class strife, life was shot through with glory. Mrs. Barrett in her sordid little tenement flat finished her breakfast dishes at ten o'clock in the morning and got down on her knees and prayed to God. ❦

Chapter Two
From Union Square to Rome

THE POWER OF HIS NAME

Tomorrow I go to Staten Island to my daughter's to babysit for a weekend, so that David and Tamar can be present at the wedding of his youngest sister in Washington, D.C. What a joy that will be. Last time I was there, Susie, six, was showing me how she could read from her first reader and the word "Jesus" kept coming up. And while she read I thought of what the theologian Bulgakoff wrote once that many Orthodox believe that the very saying of God's name invokes his presence; and I thought too of Catherine of Genoa kissing the mouth of a plague-stricken patient who repeated the Holy Name after her. What is that St. Bernard says? Jesus is music on the lips, honey in the mouth, and a shout of joy in the heart.

The Catholic Worker
April 1953

PRAYERS FOR THE DYING

"My soul hath thirsted after the strong living God; when shall I come and appear before the face of God?" But the psalmist also says, "In death there is no one that is mindful of thee." So it made me happy that I could be with my mother the last few weeks of her life, and for the last ten days at her bedside daily and hourly. Sometimes I thought to myself that it was like being present at a birth to sit by a dying person and see their intentness on what is happening to them. It almost seems that one is absorbed in a struggle, a fearful, grim, physical struggle, to breathe, to swallow, to live. And so, I kept thinking to myself, how necessary it is for one of their loved ones to be beside them, to pray for them, to offer up prayers for them unceasingly, as well as to do all those little offices one can. When my daughter was a little tiny girl, she said to me once, "When I get to be a great big woman and you are a little tiny girl, I'll take care of you," and I thought of that when I had to feed my mother by the spoonful and urge her to eat her custard. How good God was to me, to let me be there. I had prayed so constantly that I would be beside her when she died; for years, I had offered up that prayer. And God granted it quite literally. I was there, holding her hand, and she just turned her head and sighed. That was her last breath, that little sigh: and her hand was warm in mine for a long time after. ༄

The Catholic Worker
November 1945

Love and Responsibility

A Glimpse of God's Love

It was human love that helped me to understand divine love. Human love at its best, unselfish, glowing, illuminating our days, gives us a glimpse of the love of God for man. Love is the best thing we can know in this life, but it must be sustained by an effort of the will. It is not just an emotion, a warm feeling of gratification. It must lie still and quiet, dull and smoldering, for periods. It grows through suffering and patience and compassion. We must suffer for those we love, we must endure their trials and their sufferings, we must even take upon ourselves the penalties due their sins. Thus we learn to understand the love of God for His creatures. Thus we understand the Crucifixion.

It is hard to explain. It is difficult to make myself clear. If St. Paul, to whom Christ Himself spoke, saw things as through a glass, darkly, how can I hope to make things clear to you? I have only tried to put down what I do understand, urging you again not to discredit Christianity because of the faults of Christians.

Perhaps you will not see my point at all as you read this, but I pray that you too will be led by the Holy Ghost from darkness into light. Even the little I see is light to me in the darkest of days and hours. And I could not breathe or live without that light which I have now— the light of Faith which has been given to me by a merciful God Who is the Light of the world. ◈

Chapter Twelve
From Union Square to Rome

LOVE INCLUDES JUSTICE

All action springs from love. That was what Dante said. "Our God is a consuming fire," St. Paul said. One is driven, when one loves, to ways of expressing that love, to physical expressions of love, to a desire for union with others, and this love may find its expression in picket lines, in articles and speeches, crying out against injustice, destitution, and violence. It is a work of mercy to rebuke the sinner, to comfort the afflicted, to enlighten the ignorant. We must choose what means we can, and they must be pure means.

St. Paul wrote, "Know ye not that you are the temple of God and that the Spirit of God dwelleth in you? But if any man violate the temple of God, him shall God destroy. For the temple of God is holy, which you are." What reverence we must have for our brothers, for the bodies of our brothers, and what consuming care we should have that they receive what is needful, that they not be exploited.

As for ourselves, yes, we must be meek, bear injustice, malice, rash judgment. We must turn the other cheek, give up our cloak, go a second mile. . . .

We know that we can do little, but we must resolve to do all. To give ourselves completely, without reserve, to offer ourselves, to be willing to lay down our lives for our brothers. We must pray to want to. We must pray to become men of desires, and those desires will overflow into action.

It is not a counsel of perfection—this call to love. "A new precept I give unto you, to the laying down of one's life for his friend." This was a physical fact in Christ's life and should be a physical fact in our own. If we are afraid, we must pray not to be afraid, to be fools for Christ. Love includes justice. ✺

The Catholic Worker
July-August 1952

THE UPSIDE-DOWN TEACHING OF THE GOSPEL

This is the month of the Sacred Heart, the symbol of Christ's love for man. We are supposed to love as Christ loved, to the extent of laying down our lives for our brothers. That was the new commandment. To love to the extent of laying down our lives, dying to ourselves. To accept the least place, to sit back, to ask nothing for ourselves, to serve each other, to lay down our lives for our brothers, this is the strange upside-down teaching of the gospel.

We knew a priest once, a most lovable soul, and a perfect fool for Christ. Many of his fellow priests laughed at him and said, "Why, he lines up even the insane and baptizes them. He has no judgment!" He used to visit the Negro hospital in St. Louis, and night and day found him wandering through the wards. One old Negro said to me, "Whenever I opens my eyes, there is Father!" He was forever hovering over his children to dispense the sacraments. It was all he had to give. He couldn't change the rickety old hospital, he couldn't provide them with decent housing, he could not see that they got better jobs. He couldn't even seem to do much about making them give up liquor and women and gambling—but he could love them, and love them all, he did. And he gave them Everything he had. He gave them Christ. Some of his friends used to add, "whether they wanted Him or not!" But assuredly they wanted his love and they saw Christ in him when they saw his love for them. Many times I have been reminded of this old priest of St. Louis, this old Jesuit, when I have visited prisons and hospitals for the insane. It's hard to visit the chaplains and ask their help very often. They have thousands to take care of, and too often they take the view that "it's no use." "What's the use of going to that ward—or to that jail? They won't listen to you."

If one loves enough one is importunate, one repeats his love as he repeats his Hail Marys on his rosary. ∽

The Catholic Worker
June 1946

THE PRESENT STRUGGLE

It is so hard to find a balance.

We have the knowledge that this life is a passageway to another fuller life which is to come, that we are heirs to a richness and a joy beyond all telling, and that we are working toward a new heaven and a new earth, where all is love and peace, where justice dwells. We also know that what we do now will count, that we are exercising our faculties to this end, and that, although sometimes our work seems futile and without result in these fields of justice and peace and love (Ammon's work for peace, Charlie's work with teenagers, Pat's with the Ninth Street kids, and all of ours at Spring Street and at the farm), we know that is all preparation, like that of a farmer, and God will give the results, the increase, the crop. If we do not do this work, we are dead souls, no matter how vital our bodies, and there is no health in us.

We also know that religion, as the Marxists have always insisted, has, too often, like an opiate, tended to put people to sleep to the reality and the need for the present struggle for peace and justice.

"The future is so glorious in the world that is to come, why worry about the present? If we are heirs to the Kingdom, why worry about the destitution and squalor and destruction around us? To the devil with this world!" But, this world is God's world and we have no right to consign it to the devil. We should be fighting like mad against the perverse will of men, and this fight is for love of God and for love of men, the very least of them, the most unworthy of them, even to the greatest sinners among them, remembering how Jesus said from the cross, from His torture and death, "Father forgive them, for they know not what they do!" Forgive these murderers! It costs a lot to forgive murderers, every drop of our blood, every ounce of our energy. ∽

The Catholic Worker
November 1959

NOTHING ELSE BUT CHRIST

Whenever I groan within myself and think how hard it is to keep writing about love in these times of tension and strife which may at any moment become for us all a time of terror [due to the nuclear arms race], I think to myself, "What else is the world interested in? What else do we all want, each one of us, except to love and be loved, in our families, in our work, in all our relationships. God is Love. Love casts out fear. Even the most ardent revolutionist, seeking to change the world, to overturn the tables of the money changers, is trying to make a world where it is easier for people to love, to stand in that relationship with each other of love. We want with all our hearts to love, to be loved. And not just in the family but to look upon all as our mothers, sisters, brothers, children. It is when we love the most intensely and most humanly, that we can recognize how tepid is our love for others. The keenness and intensity of love brings with it suffering, of course, but joy too because it is a foretaste of heaven. I often think in relation to my love for little Beckie, Susie and Eric [her grandchildren]: "That is the way I must love every child and want to serve them, cherish them and protect them." Even that relationship which is set off from other loves by that slight change in phraseology (instead of "loving," one is "in love")—the very change in terminology, denoting a living in love, a dwelling in love at all times, being bathed in love, so that every waking thought, word, deed and suffering is permeated by that love—yes, that relationship above all should give us not only a taste of the love of God for us, but the kind of love we should have for all.

When you love people, you see all the good in them, all the Christ in them. God sees Christ, His

Son, in us and loves us. And so we should see Christ in others, *and nothing else*, and love them. There can never be enough of it. There can never be enough thinking about it. ❧

The Catholic Worker
April 1948

NOW I HAVE BEGUN

We have to go ahead and think in terms of a third way, not just those two alternatives, capitalism or communism, or my country or the fellowship of all men. We have to begin to see what Christianity really is, that "our God is a living fire; though He slay me yet will I trust him." We have to think in terms of the Beatitudes and the Sermon on the Mount and have this readiness to suffer. "We have not yet resisted unto blood." We have not yet loved our neighbor with the kind of love that is a precept to the extent of laying down our life for him. And our life very often means our money, money that we have sweated for; it means our bread, our daily living, our rent, our clothes. We haven't shown ourselves ready to lay down our life. This is a new precept, it is a new way, it is the new man we are supposed to become. I always comfort myself by saying that Christianity is only two days old (a thousand years are as one day in the sight of God), and so it is only a couple of days that are past and now it is about time we began to take these things literally, to begin tomorrow morning and say, "Now I have begun." ❧

The Catholic Worker
April 1968

THE MOST IMPORTANT THING

This is being written down at the county court where I am waiting for the commitment clerk to come down from the Bellevue psychopathic ward. The paper must go to press today, but there is a work of mercy to be done. One of our women has fallen into the hands of the state (and the state is becoming an inexorable guardian), and they have decided she is psychopathic and needs to be committed to the Manhattan Hospital. It is to rescue her that I am here—to plead to the judge to release her in our care. She had been with us six months and we had known her and helped her for some two years before that. What peculiarities she has we can cope with, but aside from any mental disorder, perhaps the result of cruel hardship and loneliness and insecurity, we are convinced that a most grave injustice is being done which we must prevent.

Right now I should be down at the printer's overseeing the makeup of the paper, because Bill Callahan, our managing editor, who of all the crowd is best at makeup, is away, and John Cort and Eddie Priest, though they can get a story and write one—though they fit in every other way into the scheme of life of *The Catholic Worker*—are not as yet at ease in writing heads and balancing the front page. Not that I am so hot myself. But I should be there, I think fretfully.

However, I shall sit and wait, and as to how things are going in the crowded print shop where three other papers are going to press at the same time—I shall just have to leave that to the Lord, and our inexperienced fellow workers. When it comes to choosing which is the most important work this morning—one human being is of greater importance than all the papers ever published—I am sure our readers agree. So when they find errors in the proofreading or in the heads, an unbalanced job in the putting together of the paper, they will excuse us. ❧

Chapter Ten
House of Hospitality

THE GIFT OF FREEDOM

We are not organized as an institution of any kind and the city does not know how to classify us. We are not a multiple dwelling, a rest home, a convalescent home, a shelter or an asylum or a convent. We are a group of people living together under one roof with one head, which is Charlie McCormack, now that Tom Sullivan has gone to the Trappists. Often I am considered to be the head, being older and the publisher of the paper. I get the summonses, the complaints. We are not registered as a charitable agency, it has been pointed out. But we hope our dear Lord recognizes us as charitable people. We try to keep the laws and regulations about housing, health, fire prevention, and take as good care of our family as we can. But we find we are always coming up against some ordinance, some infraction. We will always be in trouble with the city and the state because though we also consider ourselves good citizens and lovers of our country as well as children of God and try to bear our share of the responsibility of brother for brother, the city and the state have come to feel that this is their field (since it has been left to them). A western bishop said to me once that he did not believe in state ownership of the indigent. God wants man's free service, his freely bestowed love. So we protest and cry out against every infringement of that great gift of God, freedom, our greatest gift, after the gift of life.

That love of brother, that care for his freedom is what causes us to go into such controversial subjects as man and the state, war and peace. The implications of the gospel teaching of the works of mercy lead us into conflict with the powers of this world. Our love of God is a consuming fire. It is a fearful thing to fall into the hands of the living God. It is a living God and a living faith that we are trying to express. We are called to be holy, that is, whole men, in this life of ours. We are trying to follow this call.

The Catholic Worker
November 1955

WE ARE ALL BROTHERS

With the May issue of the paper we are beginning our nineteenth year. And with this beginning we wish to state again our faith, in this our life here on earth, that *All men are brothers*. It is our faith, our conviction, and we do state it again solemnly, in regard to Russians, Chinese, Indians, all the people of the east and the west, and we must treat them so, and love them so. It is only in this way that we can show our love for God. To love God and to love our brother as Christ loved him, to the laying down of His life for him—this is the great command, and Christ also said, "Do this and thou shalt live." It is because of this affirmation that we write as we do in *The Catholic Worker* month after month, year after year, and why we tell of houses of hospitality, farming groups, retreat houses on the land, and the works of mercy that are the life of these communities. It is not enough to say it, to repeat it, to hear it sing in our hearts, as in that great chorus in the last movement of the Ninth Symphony of Beethoven. It must be translated into act, into flesh and blood, into our eating and drinking and working and loving.

The Catholic Worker
May 1951

5

Mission

RECONSTRUCTING
THE SOCIAL ORDER

From the first issue of The Catholic Worker:

To Our Readers:

For those who are sitting on park benches in the warm spring sunlight.

For those who are huddling in shelters trying to escape the rain.

For those who are walking the streets in the all but futile search for work.

For those who think that there is no hope for the future, no recognition of their plight—this little paper is addressed.

It is printed to call their attention to the fact that the Catholic Church has a social program—to let them know that there are men of God who are working not only for their spiritual, but for their material welfare.

It's time there was a Catholic paper printed for the unemployed.

The fundamental aim of most radical sheets is the conversion of its readers to radicalism and atheism.

Is it not possible to be radical and not atheist?

Is it not possible to protest, to expose, to complain, to point out abuses and demand reforms without desiring the overthrow of religion?

In an attempt to popularize and make known the encyclicals of the popes in regard to social justice and the program put forth by the Church for the "reconstruction of the social order," this news sheet, *The Catholic Worker*, is started.

It is not as yet known whether it will be a monthly, a fortnightly, or a weekly. It all depends on the funds collected for the printing and distribution. Those who can subscribe, and those who can donate, are asked to do so.

This first number of *The Catholic Worker* was planned, written, and edited in the kitchen of a tenement on Fifteenth Street, on subway platforms, on the "L," the ferry. There is no editorial office, no overhead in the way of telephone or electricity, no salaries paid.

The money for the printing of the first issue was raised by begging small contributions from friends. A colored priest in Newark sent us ten dollars and the prayers of his congregation. A colored sister in New Jersey, garbed also in holy poverty, sent us a dollar. Another kindly and generous friend sent twenty-five.

The rest of it the editors squeezed out of their own earnings, and at that they were using money necessary to pay milk bills, gas bills, electric light bills.

By accepting delay the utilities did not know that they were furthering the cause of social justice. They were, for the time being, unwitting cooperators.

Next month someone may donate us an office. Who knows?

It is cheering to remember that Jesus Christ wandered this earth with no place to lay His head. *The foxes have holes and the birds of the air their nests, but the Son of Man has no place to lay His head.* And when we consider our fly-by-night existence, our uncertainty, we remember (with pride at sharing the honor), that the disciples supped by the seashore and wandered through corn fields picking the ears from the stalks wherewith to make their frugal meals. ❧

> *The Catholic Worker*
> May 1933

On Earth As It is in Heaven

For the sake of new readers, for the sake of men on our bread lines, for the sake of the employed and unemployed, the organized and unorganized workers, and also for the sake of ourselves, we must reiterate again and again what are our aims and purposes.

Together with the works of mercy, feeding, clothing and sheltering our brothers, we must indoctrinate. We must "give reason for the faith that is in us." Otherwise, we are scattered members of the Body of Christ, we are not "all members one of another." Otherwise, our religion is an opiate, for ourselves alone, for our comfort or for our individual safety or indifferent custom.

We cannot live alone. We cannot go to heaven alone. Otherwise, as Péguy said, God will say to us, "Where are the others?" (This is in one sense only as, of course, we believe that we must be what we would have the other fellow be. We must look to ourselves, our own lives first.)

If we do not keep indoctrinating, we lose the vision. And if we lose the vision, we become merely philanthropists, doling out palliatives.

The vision is this. We are working for "a new heaven and a new *earth*, wherein justice dwelleth." We are trying to say with action, "Thy will be done on *earth* as it is in heaven." We are working for a Christian social order. ❧

The Catholic Worker
February 1940

Revolution of the Heart

The greatest challenge of the day is: how to bring about a revolution of the heart, a revolution which has to start with each one of us? When we begin to take the lowest place, to wash the feet of others, to love our brothers with that burning love, that passion, which led to the cross, then we can truly say, "Now I have begun."

Day after day we accept our failure, but we accept it because of our knowledge of the victory of the cross. God has given us our vocation, as He gave it to the small boy who contributed his few loaves and fishes to help feed the multitude, and which Jesus multiplied so that He fed five thousand people.

Loaves and fishes! How much we owe to God in praise, honor, thanksgiving!

Chapter Nineteen
Loaves and Fishes

A Choice of Technique

Our cash box is empty. We just collected the last pennies for a ball of twine and stamps and we shall take a twenty-five-cent subscription which just came in to buy meat for a stew for supper. But the printing bill, the one hundred and sixty-five dollars of it which remains unpaid, confronts us and tries to intimidate us.

But what is one hundred and sixty-five dollars to St. Joseph, or to St. Teresa of Avila either? We refuse to be affrighted. (Though of course the printer may be, "Oh, he of little faith!")

Don Bosco tells lots of stories about needing this sum or that sum to pay rent and other bills with and the money arriving miraculously on time. And he too was always in need, always asking, and always receiving.

A great many of our friends urge us to put our paper on a business-like basis. But this isn't a business, it's a movement. And we don't know anything about business around here anyway. Well-meaning friends say, "But people get tired of appeals." We don't believe it. Probably most of our friends live as we do, from day to day and from hand to mouth, and as they get, they are willing to give. So we shall continue to appeal and we know that the paper will go on.

It's a choice of technique, after all. People call up offering us the services of their organizations to raise money. They have lists, they send out telephone and mail appeals. They are business-like and most coldly impersonal. Though they may be successful in raising funds for Jewish, Catholic, and Protestant organizations and offer us several thousand a week, minus their commission, we can't warm up to these tactics. We learn ours from the gospels and what's good enough for St. Peter and St. Paul is good enough for us. Their technique of revolution was the technique of Christ and it's the one to go back to. ∞

Chapter One
House of Hospitality

WE DID NOT CHOOSE THIS WORK

One reason I feel sure of the rightness of the path we are traveling in our work is that we did not pick it out ourselves. In those beautiful verses in the twenty-fifth chapter of St. Matthew, Jesus tells us that we must feed the hungry, and shelter those without homes and visit the sick and the prisoner. We cannot feel too satisfied with the way we are doing our work—there is too much of it; we have more than our share, you might say. Yet we can say, "If that's the way He wants it—"

I say we did not choose this work, and that is true. So it was with each of us. John Cort thought he was coming to us to study and work with the problem of labor unions and he found himself "running a flophouse," as he said. I, being a journalist, looked to editing and publishing a paper each month, writing what I chose, and not being subject to any publisher. But because we wrote about the obligations of those who call themselves Christians and who try "stripping yourselves of the old man with his deeds and putting on the new," as St. Paul said, it is as though we were each being admonished, "All right, if you believe as you say, do it."

One time, as I was standing at the window of our farmhouse at Newburgh, I saw a man coming down the road with a suitcase. "He is probably coming here," I sighed. Another member of the family turned to me accusingly and said, "Then you don't mean what you say in *The Catholic Worker!*"

"Is this what you meant, Peter [Maurin]? I asked him once about an overcrowded house of hospitality.

"Well," he hesitated. "At least it arouses the conscience."

Which is something. ❧

Chapter Seventeen
Loaves and Fishes

WHO'S COUNTING?

This last year, at St. Joseph's House of Hospitality, we gave out, roughly speaking and underestimating it at that, 460,000 meals. Also 18,250 nights' lodging. This is what the world sees and if we wished to impress the world we would multiply this by eighteen years, and the figures would be truly impressive.

But suppose a mother should say, in a plea for sympathy, "I've put one thousand and ninety-five meals on the table this last year. I've washed fifty thousand plates."

It is easy to see how foolish it is to look at things in this light, in this *big way*. I am sure that God is not counting the meals. He is looking at Tony Aratari, Joe Monroe, Ray Taylor, turning off their alarm clocks at five every morning to go downstairs to start the coffee, cut the bread. They get no credit for being noble. They have no realization of dying to themselves, of giving up their lives. They are more often than not abused by friends and relatives for not getting jobs, using their education, "supporting themselves," instead of living on charity. "This then is perfect joy," as St. Francis would say. ✑

The Catholic Worker
January 1951

THE LITTLE WAY

When a mother, a housewife, asks what she can do, one can only point to the way of St. Thérèse, that little way, so much misunderstood and so much despised. She did all for the love of God, even to putting up with the irritation in herself caused by the proximity of a nervous nun. She began with working for peace in her own heart, and willing to love where love was difficult, and so she grew in love, and increased the sum total of love in the world, not to speak of peace.

[John Henry] Newman wrote: "Let us but raise the level of religion in our hearts, and it will rise in the world.

He who attempts to set up God's kingdom in his heart, furthers it in the world." And this goes for the priest, too, wherever he is, whether he deals with the problem of war or with poverty. He may write and speak, but he needs to study the little way, which is all that is available to the poor, and the only alternative to the mass approach of the state. Missionaries throughout the world recognize this little way of cooperatives and credit unions, small industry, village commune and cottage economy. And not only missionaries. Down in our own South, in the Delta regions among the striking farmers of Mississippi, this "little way" is being practiced and should be studied. ∾

The Catholic Worker
December 1965

IN SEARCH OF LOST SHEEP

Jacques Maritain, speaking at a Catholic Worker meeting a few years ago, urged us to read the gospels. Thérèse of Lisieux, the little saint of our day, carried it next to her heart. Even if we read only the gospel for Sunday, several times, God sends us a special message for our need.

I thought of that a few Sundays ago as I read the parable about the lost sheep. Certainly the men around the Bowery are lost sheep. They are our brothers in Jesus; He died for each of them. What respect we should feel for them!

When we began the Catholic Worker, we first thought of it as a headquarters for the paper, a place for round-table discussions, for learning crafts, for studying ways of building up a new social order. But God has made it much more than all this. He has made it a place for the poor. They come early in the morning from their beds in cheap flophouses, from the benches in the park across the street, from the holes and corners of the city. They are the most destitute, the most abandoned.

It is easy for people to see Jesus in the children of the slums, and institutions and schools are built to help them. That is a vocation in itself. But these abandoned men are looked upon as hopeless. "No good will come of it." We are contributing to laziness. We are feeding people who won't work. These are the accusations made. God help us, we give them so little: bread and coffee in the morning, soup and bread at noon. Two scant meals.

We are a family of forty or fifty at the Catholic Worker. We keep emphasizing that. But we are also a House of Hospitality. So many come that it is impossible to give personal attention to each one; we can only give what we have, in the name of Jesus. Thank God for directing our vocation. We did not choose this work. He sent it to us. We will always, please God, be clambering around the rocks and briars, the barrenness, the fruitlessness of city life, in search of lost sheep.

The Catholic Worker
July-August 1953

THE ANSWER TO OUR PRESENT AGONY

One of our readers, and a most dear friend, has been carrying on the work of sending packages to cold and hungry Europe. She realizes most keenly that the only answer to our present agony is the *personal* application of Christian principles. It is necessary to do the thing one's self. If people are hungry, how can we eat? If they are cold, how can we go clothed and sheltered? It is easy to see why the saints espoused voluntary poverty. "The coat that hangs in our closet belongs to the poor," one of the early fathers said. . . .

Europe and Asia are cold and hungry. What can we do about it? We may say that there is nothing that we can do, but that is not true. We can send clothes, *personally*; food, *personally*. There is a simple way to reach individuals in Europe, and that is through the great Catholic sisterhoods who have houses all over the world. There are nuns all around us of every nationality, and if you go to them and ask for the addresses of orphanages and hospitals and convents in Italy, France, Belgium, Holland, and many other countries, you can send bundles up to eleven pounds. Down here in this Italian neighborhood, the barber next door has sent seventy packages containing food and clothing. Through his relatives here, he is helping his relatives there. They are working in *the little way*; that way for our time; that way recommended and taught and practiced by the Little Flower. (That was her great message to us today.)

We should rejoice that there is work for us today, that we can put forth our hands to strong things.

In these days of sore distress our happiness and our love will be in doing these things, and in doing these things we will find God and find happiness. ❧

The Catholic Worker
November 1945

THE GREAT FAILURE

I know that I will give much satisfaction to many of our fellow workers when I admit that we have failed and that on every front. We have failed to clarify thought and probably will till the end of our days. We have failed in running houses of hospitality, in that they are not indoctrination centers and places to teach "cult, culture, and cultivation" as Peter [Maurin] wanted, and all our time is taken up with the immediate practice of the works of mercy there. We have failed in establishing farming groups, whether as agronomic universities, or farming communes of families. This is in spite of the fact that we have fourteen houses and eight farms around the country associated with the Catholic Worker, with these ideas, or some of them. The houses flourish in that there are always the indigent, the destitute, the poor to flock to our doors. There is plenty of obvious work being done and far more than enough to keep every hand and heart busy. But have we even begun to build the new social order that Peter envisioned?

About all the above failures, I must say that I am not much concerned. I think that such failures are inseparable to a work of this kind, and necessary for our growth in holiness. Such failure, for those of us who have dedicated our lives to this work, is our cross. As a matter of fact, our failure is so continuous that we never think of it, we just go on working, without judging ourselves, as St. Paul tells us to. We can list our accomplishments as glorious examples of God's providence, and of our faith in it. We grow in faith in it and in our very persistence, we are growing in hope and charity. God grant that we persevere. ❧

The Catholic Worker
January 1954

6

Christ in One Another

THE ONLY FITTING WORSHIP

Only by nourishing ourselves as we have been bidden to do by Christ, by eating His Body and drinking His Blood, can we become Christ and put on the new man.

These are great mysteries. Most of the time we do not comprehend at all. Sometimes the Holy Spirit blows upon us and chases some of the fog away and we see a bit more clearly. But most of the time we see through a glass darkly. Our need to worship, to praise, to give thanksgiving, makes us return to the Mass daily, as the only fitting worship which we can offer to God. Having received our God in the consecrated bread and wine, which still to sense is bread and wine, it is now not we ourselves who do these things except by virtue of the fact that we will to do them, and put ourselves in the position to do them by coming to the Holy Sacrifice, receiving communion, and then with Christ in our hearts and literally within us in the bread we have received, giving this praise, honor, and glory and thanksgiving.

How inadequate words are to say these things, to write them. ◯

The Catholic Worker
September 1962

THE MYSTICAL BODY OF CHRIST

We believe in the brotherhood of man and the Fatherhood of God. This teaching, the doctrine of the Mystical Body of Christ, involves today the issue of unions (where men call each other brothers); it involves the racial question; it involves cooperatives, credit unions, crafts; it involves houses of hospitality and farming communes. It is with all these means that we can live as though we believed indeed that we are all members one of another, knowing that when "the health of one member suffers, the health of the whole body is lowered."

This work of ours toward a new heaven and a new earth shows a correlation between the material and the spiritual, and, of course, recognizes the primacy of the spiritual. Food for the body is not enough. There must be food for the soul. Hence the leaders of the work, and as many as we can induce to join us, must go daily to Mass, to receive food for the soul. And as our perceptions are quickened, and as we pray that our faith be increased, we will see Christ in each other, and we will not lose faith in those around us, no matter how stumbling their progress is. It is easier to have faith that God will support each House of Hospitality and Farming Commune and supply our needs in the way of food and money to pay bills, than it is to keep a strong, hearty, living faith in each individual around us—to see Christ in him. If we lose faith, if we stop the work of indoctrinating, we are in a way denying Christ again.

We must practice the presence of God. He said that when two or three are gathered together, there He is in the midst of them. He is with us in our kitchens, at our tables, on our bread lines, with our visitors, on our farms. When we pray for our material needs, it brings us close to His humanity. He, too, needed food and shelter. He, too, warmed His hands at a fire and lay down in a boat to sleep.

When we have spiritual reading at meals, when we have the rosary at night, when we have study groups, forums, when we go out to distribute literature at meetings, or sell it on the street corners, Christ is there with us. What we do is very little. But it is like the little boy with a few loaves and fishes. Christ took that little and increased it. He will do the rest. What we do is so little we may seem to be constantly failing. But so did He fail. He met with apparent failure on the cross. But unless the seed fall into the earth and die, there is no harvest. ❧

The Catholic Worker
February 1940

A ROOM FOR CHRIST

Some time ago I saw the death notice of a sergeant-pilot who had been killed on active service. After the usual information, a message was added which, I imagine, is likely to be initiated. It said that anyone who had ever known the dead boy would always be sure of a welcome at his parents' home. So, even now that the war is over, the father and mother will go on taking in strangers for the simple reason that they will be reminded of their dead son by the friends he made.

That is rather like the custom that existed among the first generations of Christians, when faith was a bright fire that warmed more than those who kept it burning. In every house then a room was kept ready for any stranger who might ask for shelter; it was even called "the strangers' room." And this not because these people, like the parents of the dead airman, thought they could trace something of someone they loved in the stranger who used it, not because the man or woman to whom they gave shelter reminded them of Christ, but because— plain and simple and stupendous fact—he was Christ.

It would be foolish to pretend that it is easy always to remember this. If everyone were holy and handsome, with "alter Christus" shining in neon lighting from them, it would be easy to see Christ in everyone. If Mary had appeared in Bethlehem clothed, as St. John says, with the sun, a crown of twelve stars on her head and the moon under her feet, then people would have fought to make room for her. But that was not God's way for her nor is it Christ's way for Himself now when He is disguised under every type of humanity that treads the earth. ❧

The Catholic Worker
December 1945

LOVING THE CHRIST IN OTHERS

Peter [Maurin] made you feel a sense of his mission as soon as you met him. He did not begin by tearing down, or by painting so intense a picture of misery and injustice that you burned to change the world. Instead, he aroused in you a sense of your own capacities for work, for accomplishment. He made you feel that you and all men had great and generous hearts with which to love God. If you once recognized this fact in yourself you would expect and find it in others. "The art of human contacts," Peter called it happily. But it was seeing Christ in others, loving the Christ you saw in others. Greater than this, it was having faith in the Christ in others without being able to see Him. Blessed is he that believes without seeing. ∾

Part Three
The Long Loneliness

To Die for Love

The love of God and man become the love of equals as the love of the bride and the bridegroom is the love of equals, and not the love of the sheep for the shepherd, or the servant for the master, or the son for the father. We may stand at times in the relationship of servant, and at other times in that of son, as far as our feelings go and in our present state. But the relationship to which we hope to attain, is that of the love of the Canticle of Canticles. If we cannot deny the *self* in us, kill the self love, as He has commanded, and put on the Christ life, then God will do it for us. We must become like Him. Love must go through purgations. ∾

The Catholic Worker
September 1948

The Least of My Brethren

My criticism of Christians in the past, and it *still* holds good of too many of them, is that they in fact deny God and reject Him. "Amen I say to you, as long as you did it to one of these my least brethren, you did it to me" (Matthew 25:40), Christ said, and today there are Christians who affront Christ in the Negro, in the poor Mexican, the Italian, yes and the Jew. Catholics believe that man is the temple of the Holy Ghost, that he is made to the image and likeness of God. We believe that of Jew and Gentile. We believe that all men are members or potential members of the Mystical Body of Christ and since there is no time with God, we must so consider each man whether he is atheist, Jew or Christian.

You ask do we really believe it, when we see our fellows herded like brutes in municipal lodging houses, tramping the streets and roads hungry, working at starvation wages or under an inhuman speed-up, living in filthy degrading conditions. Seeing many Christians denying Him, hating Him in the poor, is it any wonder a heresy has sprung up denying Him in word and deed?

The first commandment is that we should love the Lord our God. We can only show our love for God by our love for our fellows. "If any man say, I love God, and hateth his brother he is a liar. For he that loveth not his brother, whom he seeth, how can he love God, whom he seeth not?" (1 John 4: 20). ❧

Chapter Twelve
From Union Square to Rome

CHRIST WAS A WORKER

While I was in Los Angeles, a young couple came to our place carrying a month-old baby and leading another eighteen months old. Some kindly worker had given them a lift on the last lap of their journey and turned his room over to them since he worked nights and could sleep days. That traveler, the father of the two little ones, was also a carpenter. Did anyone see Joseph in this unemployed man? Did they see the Holy Family, epitomized in this little group? Did they see Christ in the worker who helped them?

Christ was a worker and in the three years He roamed through Palestine He had no place to lay His head. But He said, "Take no thought for what ye shall eat and where ye shall sleep, or what ye shall put on. Seek ye first the Kingdom of God and His righteousness and all these things shall be added unto you. . . . For your Heavenly Father knoweth that you have need of these things."

For one year now, our coffee line has been going on. Right now we are making seventy-five gallons of coffee every morning. There are too many of you for us, who wait on the line, to talk to you. We must think of the other fellow waiting out in the cold, as you remember, for you are very prompt in finishing your breakfast and making way for them. It is a grim and desperate struggle to keep the line going in more ways than one.

It is hard, I repeat, to talk to you of religion. But without faith in each other, we cannot go on. Without hope we cannot go on. Without hope we cannot live. To those who are without hope, I remind you of Christ, your brother. Religion, thought in terms of our brotherhood through Christ, is not the opiate of the people. It is a battle "mighty to God unto the pulling down of fortifications." Do not let either capitalist or communist kill this noble instinct in you. ∾

> *The Catholic Worker*
> December 1937

GOD IN OUR HEARTS

Teresa [Day's Daughter], aged seven, is very much around the office these first cold days. Since *The Catholic Worker* has moved to the store downstairs, there is ample room for another assistant and her little desk.

She likes even better than sitting at a desk to crawl under the furniture coverings of a set of chairs and sofa the young woman racktender at the Paulist church sent down as a contribution to our office furniture. There, ensconced in her tent with her little friend Freddy Rubino, I heard her talking the other day.

"There now," she said, "you have committed a mortal sin, and you haven't got God in your heart any more."

Freddy is two years younger than herself. Freddy had a few minutes before kicked his mother in the shins and called her a pig and generally scandalized the neighborhood, though everyone should have been accustomed to witnessing these scenes at least once a day.

Teresa's reproof made Freddy indignant. "He is so there," he insisted. "He's right there."

"No, there's a devil there now."

"I don't want a devil there. I want God there. He is there."

"Well, all you have to do is to say you're sorry and it will be all right."

So that was settled. ❦

Chapter One
House of Hospitality

1

Work

A Philosophy of Work

Peter [Maurin's] Christian philosophy of work was this. God is our creator. God made us in His image and likeness. Therefore we are creators. He gave us a garden to till and cultivate. We become co-creators by our responsible acts, whether in bringing forth children, or producing food, furniture, or clothing. The joy of creativeness should be ours.

But because of the Fall the curse is laid on us of having to earn our bread by the sweat of our brows, in labor. St. Paul said that since the Fall, nature itself travaileth and groaneth. So man has to contend with fallen nature in the beasts and in the earth as well as in himself. But when he overcomes the obstacles, he attains again to the joy of creativity. Work is not then all pain and drudgery.

Part Three
The Long Loneliness

WORK AS A GIFT

On the farm there is plenty of work for all; another reason why Peter was always extolling the land. People cannot live without working. Work is as necessary as bread. But what is needed is a philosophy of work. Work is a gift, a vocation. Before the Fall, Adam was given the garden to cultivate. It was only after the Fall that all nature travailed and groaned so that man has to work with the sweat of his brow and combat earthquakes, floods, droughts, boll weevils, Japanese beetles, fatigue and sloth. We have to recognize work as a penance, but we must also recognize work as a gift. Man has talents which God has given him, and he must develop these talents. He must find the work he can do best, and then learn to do it well, for his own sake and the sake of his fellows.

Peter's indoctrinations about scholars and workers has this practical result around the houses of hospitality. When the scholar starts scrubbing and cleaning house, the cooperation from the worker is more willing, more spontaneous. Everyone wants to help. The labor and exercise tends to relieve the discouragement that often threatens to encompass the scholar. He understands better after a bout with a mop the discouragements of the poor man, his slothfulness, his hopelessness. He begins, too, to understand what Christ meant when He said He came to minister, not to be ministered unto. He begins to understand the humiliations of the very poor, and by seeking them voluntarily he finds peace and rest in them. "My yoke is easy and my burden light." "The meek shall inherit the earth." But these things are not understood until practiced. St. Francis said, "You cannot know what you have not practiced." ∽

The Catholic Worker
September 1945

DO WHAT COMES TO HAND

Today we are not contented with little achievements, with small beginnings. We should look to St. Thérèse, the Little Flower, to walk her little way, her way of love. We should look to St. Teresa of Avila who was not content to be like those people who proceeded with the pace of hens about God's business, but like those people who on their own account were greatly daring in what they wished to do for God. It is we ourselves that we have to think about, no one else. That is the way the saints worked. They paid attention to what they were doing and if others were attracted to them by their enterprise, why, well and good. But they looked to themselves first of all.

Do what comes to hand. Whatsoever thy hand finds to do, do it with all thy might. After all, God is with us. It shows too much conceit to trust to ourselves, to be discouraged at what we ourselves can accomplish. It is lacking in faith in God to be discouraged. After all, we are going to proceed with His help. We offer Him what we are going to do. If He wishes it to prosper, it will. We must depend solely on Him. Work as though everything depended on ourselves, and pray as though everything depended on God, as St. Ignatius says. ❧

Chapter Four
House of Hospitality

THE CATHOLIC RADICAL

Peter Maurin wanted to call *The Catholic Worker* The Catholic Radical because he believes in getting down to the roots. And the root of our evil, he has been crying out like a prophet, like a St. John the Baptist, is the lack of a philosophy of work.

It is significant that it is in reformatories that boys are taught crafts and trades. It is significant that it is in insane hospitals that the patients, some few of them, are taught to use their hands to do creative work.

But the sad part of it is that though they have these schools, teaching skills, and some learn to do things very well, and probably get great joy out of doing them, they do them with the sad sense of futility, of boondoggling, of having been given something to do because they are either criminal or insane—and not that they are doing things which are good and natural to man that they can continue doing when they get out, creating, making, using mind and body to work on beautiful things God has given man, raw materials He has provided, and in so working on God's good things, getting a sense of the sacramentality of life, the holiness, the symbolism of things. ❧

The Catholic Worker
November 1946

THE APOSTOLATE OF THE LAITY

We will have to go back to before the Reformation to return to the idea of apostolate of the laity. There is more anti-laicism than anti-clericalism in the country today, I am sure.

Thank God most of our priests are the sons of working men, the rector of a seminary said to me once. That is very true. But it is so easy to get out of the habit of poverty, of charity, of hospitality. St. John had to keep pleading, "my children, love one another." And in the first chapter of the Apocalypse there is the sad statement that charity had grown cold. There is always a losing of early fervor, of early charity, of early understanding. It is hard to remain as little children, and be unsuspicious, to clean the heart of all bitterness, to keep the loving spirit.

It is also true that these sons of working men have not thought out these issues, and they have not had the leadership that the workers have had in Karl Marx, in his analysis of the social order, and his condemnation of it. They have accepted this social order; they have not questioned it. They have said, "The poor you will always have with you." They have said, "Seek first the kingdom of heaven." Their great strength was also their weakness. Their conviction of heaven was so strong that they did not think this world worth bothering about. But what of their brothers—are they not worth bothering about? How can we see our brother hungry and say, "Go be thou filled" and not give to him? Charity is not enough. If he has been robbed, restoration must be made to him. God put man on this earth to work for his bread, but what if there is no work? He has been defrauded of his work, of his labor, and of the fruits of his labor. He has neither work nor property and his state is bad indeed.

There is work now. Much of our national expenditure by the government is for war, past and present. Much of this work, this labor, is not good work, constructive work, but work for preparedness, or dealing with pensions or hospitals, etc. It is not even in building homes that have been destroyed by war, let alone homes here in this country where we did not have that destruction. Slums are still with us. Many houses have been torn down, more than have been put up. Farms have been consolidated and produce less than if they were all small farms; soil has been depleted, national resources have been wasted. And are we to sit by and see man, and God's good earth, so ruined and degraded, and then be told, "Do not bother about these things, seek first the kingdom of heaven?" ∽

The Catholic Worker
March 1947

Teach Us How to Work

How to give a philosophy of work, that elusive thing Peter Maurin was always talking about. That is a problem that is always with us too. Because if fire is twice bread, as the Arabs say, work is thrice bread. It is good to write about this on St. Joseph's Day because he was a worker, on occasion homeless, a displaced person, in exile for a time, but usually with work enough for him and his Son. We know so little about him, only that he worked hard and dreamed when he was troubled, and prayed, but come to think of it, the gospel did not say anything about his praying. But with the Benedictines, work is prayer. So we need to pray to St. Joseph to teach us how to work, what to work at, and where the work is.

If we had Peter Maurin's philosophy of work, we would not need to worry. He used to say to people looking for a boss, "Fire the bosses." He used to say, "Work—not wages." He used to say, "Labor is a gift, not a commodity, to be bought and sold." All of these are hard sayings, hard to understand and to work out. But to act on them is to make a beginning in building another social order—to lay the first stone in the new city. In all these slums and skid rows of our cities, strangely enough, one sees these ideas in their faint beginnings. The man who makes a push cart out of a discarded baby carriage and collects rags, bottles, cardboard to sell for his rent money; Karl Meyer in Chicago collecting the discarded fruits and broken boxes and dented cans from the trash cans of the alleys of the Gold Coast in Chicago; Ed Forand at our place, going early mornings to the markets to get the discards and to give a token payment. And I remember too one of our early helpers, Charles Rich, who sold gardenias on the street to pay for bed and board and spent the rest of his time in our great libraries studying about God and man.

When I look around us at Chrystie Street's St. Joseph's House and at the Peter Maurin Farm, I see how many there are among us who *have* a philosophy of work, earning their own way and responding to the needs of others in all the "service" work of putting meals on the table each day, cleaning, sorting out clothes, and in endless clerical work which goes with so widespread a community as ours, a never-ending and time-consuming work.

The Catholic Worker
April 1963

8

The Church

THE WORD MUST BE UPHELD

I am thinking of what I have come to think of as fundamental to our search for peace, for non-violence. A flood of water (and Christ is living water) washes out sins—all manner of filth, degradation, fear, horror. He is also the Word. And studying the New Testament, and its commentators, I have come in this my seventy-sixth year, to think of a few holy words of Jesus as the greatest comfort of my life.

"Judge not."

"Forgive us our trespasses as we forgive those who trespass against us."

"Forgive seventy times seven times."

All words of our Lord and Savior. "I have knowledge of salvation through forgiveness of my sins," Zechariah sang in his canticle.

And so, when it comes to divorce, birth control, abortion, I must write in this way. The teaching of Christ, the Word, must be upheld. Held up though one would think that it is completely beyond us— out of our reach, impossible to follow. I believe Christ is our Truth and is with us always. We may stretch towards it, falling short, failing seventy times seven, but forgiveness is always there. He is a kind and loving judge. And so are ninety-nine percent of the priests in the confessional. The verdict there is always "not guilty" even though our "firm resolve with the help of His grace to confess our sins, do penance and amend our lives" may seem a hopeless proposition. It always contains, that act of contrition, the phrase "to confess our sins," even though we have just finished confessing them, which indicates that the priest knows, and we know, and we want to be honest about it, that we will be back in that confessional, again and again.

I believe in the Sacraments. I believe grace is conferred through the Sacraments. I believe the priest is empowered to forgive sins. Grace is defined as "participation in the divine life," so little by little we are putting off the old man and putting on the new.

Actually, "putting on Christ."

The Catholic Worker
December 1972

THEIR DEAREST HOME

It is pleasant before Mass to sit and meditate early in the morning in the little Italian Church down on Twelfth Street. On the left hand side, the open windows look out on fire escapes and roofs, green-edged with plants. Close to the church window there is corn growing in a tub, tomato plants, basil and other pots of herbs which are fragrant if you crush them between your fingers. People are leaning out of their windows already, trying to get a breath of air.

Inside the Church of Our Lady Help of Christians, the two Italian girls sing the Mass with joyous natural voices, trilling through the *Kyrie Eleison*. The priest, weighed down with his heavy robes, moves with intent stillness through the sacrifice of the Mass.

I love this church of the Salesian Fathers. It is indeed what a church should be, the center of the community. Every morning at the seven and eight o'clock Masses, both of which are sung, there is a goodly gathering of people, not just devout old ladies and old men, but many young ones too.

Before and after Mass there is always a priest hearing confessions.

Every evening from five o'clock on to past nine, people dropping in, before supper, on their way home from market, from work, from play on the streets—everyone is living on the streets these hot days. There is a crowd at the recitation of the rosary and Benediction. The whole congregation sings the hymns and litanies. And even those priests who are not on duty are there somewhere in evidence. The church is their dearest home, and they evidently love to be contemplating the Humanity of Christ, present there in the Tabernacle. ❧

Chapter Three
House of Hospitality

WE ARE ALL GUILTY

Americans hate the word obedience, and the only way to look at it is from the supernatural point of view, not from the natural, because it is often folly. This is not to deny that conscience comes first: one must obey the voice of conscience, one must obey God rather than men, as St. Peter himself was the first to say.

And here is one of those delicate problems that drive the rest of the world crazy when they observe the Catholic in his relations to Holy Mother the Church. They point out the scandals in the Church, the mistakes in history, the bad popes, the Inquisition, the lining up of the Church with temporal power, the concordats, the expediency, the diplomacy, and so on and so on.

Right under one's nose there is always plenty to complain of. Churches, schools, monasteries being built while the municipal lodging house is packed with mothers and children separated from husbands and fathers because of lack of housing; a spreading unemployment; race prejudice amongst Catholics, and priests and sisters, too; anti-Semitism—oh, yes, there is plenty of scandal.

"The just will be judged first," and the "just" is made up of the lame, the halt, and the blind because Christ came to call sinners, and the Church is full of them, in high and low places.

[Romano] Guardini said that the Church was the cross and one could not separate Christ from His cross. He said, too, that we must learn to live in a state of permanent dissatisfaction and impatience with the Church. We have to suffer and hang our heads at all the accusations made against us. We are all guilty, we all make up the Body of Christ. And we must suffer with bitterness, the Little Flower said, if need be, and without courage, and that is what makes the suffering especially keen. ✍

The Catholic Worker
December 1949

WE EAT TO SUSTAIN LIFE

It took me a long time as a convert to realize the presence of Christ as Man in the Sacrament. He is the same Jesus Who walked on earth, Who slept in the boat as the tempest arose, Who hungered in the desert, Who prayed in the garden, Who conversed with the woman by the well, Who rested at the house of Martha and Mary, Who wandered through the cornfields, picking the ears of corn to eat.

Jesus is there as Man. He is there, Flesh and Blood, Soul and Divinity. He is our leader Who is always with us. Do you wonder that Catholics are exultant in this knowledge, that their Leader is with them? "I am with you all days, even to the consummation of the world."

Christ is bread on our altars because bread is the staple of the world, the simplest thing in the world, something of which we eat and never get tired. We will always have bread whether it is corn, wheat, or rye, or whatever it is made from. We will always find wherever we go some staple which is called bread.

We eat to sustain life. It is the most elemental thing we do. For the life of the body we need food. For the life of the soul we need food. So the simplest, most loving, most thorough thing Christ could do before He died, was to institute the Blessed Sacrament. He did this by taking a piece of bread which He blessed and broke and gave to his disciples saying "Take ye and eat. This is My Body." And taking the chalice He gave thanks, and gave to them saying: "Drink ye all of this for this is My Blood." And He told them to do this in commemoration of Him.

If you sat and thought forever and ever, you could not think of any way for Christ to remain with us which would bring us closer to Him. ❧

Chapter Thirteen
From Union Square to Rome

CHRIST YEARNS FOR US

I know now that the Catholic Church is the church of the poor, no matter what you say about the wealth of her priests and bishops. I have mentioned in these pages the few Catholics I met before my conversion, but daily I saw people coming from Mass. Never did I set foot in a Catholic church but that I saw people there at home with Him. First Fridays, novenas, and missions brought the masses thronging in and out of the Catholic churches. They were of all nationalities, of all classes, but most of all they were the poor. The very attacks made against the Church proved her divinity to me. Nothing but a divine institution could have survived the betrayal of Judas, the denial of Peter, the sins of many of those who professed her Faith, who were supposed to minister to her poor.

Christ is God or He is the world's greatest liar and impostor. How can you communists who claim to revere Him as a working class leader fail to see this? And if Christ established His Church on earth with Peter as its rock, that faulty one who denied him three times, who fled from Him when he was in trouble, then I, too, wanted a share in that tender compassionate love that is so great. Christ can forgive all sins and yearn over us no matter how far we fall. ∾

Chapter One
From Union Square to Rome

CLOTHED WITH GRANDEUR

A great wave of gratitude to Holy Mother Church swept over me as I thought of the ministrations of these priests. At nine there had been the colorful and solemn and most happy occasion of all the little children of the parish making their first Holy Communion. And at ten this Mass for the dead!

All the great moments of life are here clothed with grandeur, recognition of man's dignity, his worth in the sight of God who loved him so much as to die for him. First Communion coming to young ones at a time when the desires of the flesh begin to grow, opening up their hearts to a love strong as death, showing them what love really means. St. Thérèse called her first Holy Communion "a kiss of love, a fusion." And now a requiem Mass which brought comfort to the afflicted, a sense of triumph. Death is swallowed up in victory.

I felt somewhat abashed going up to the communion rail, alone, in the midst of all the solemnity. I felt like a wayfarer, alone at the communion rail, having no immediate part as it were either with the feastings or mournings of those about me, like Lazarus at the gate, and the priests the rich men coming down to bring me food for body and soul, or rather as though God himself came with all pomp and grandeur bringing down his Son to the lowliest wayfarer, or sojourner.

The Catholic Worker
June 1954

ACCEPTANCE OF THE HUMAN CONDITION

The transcendental is thought of often as manifesting itself in signs and wonders, prophecies and voices from the dead. There is evidence of it in the miracles which take place around us, miracles which are more common than we suppose, and which the Catholic Church is very hesitant to confirm without long investigation. There may well be more of them than we know, since most of us, if a miracle were performed for us in the way of healing, would prefer not to submit to long investigation. Most of us would be reluctant to report, or even perhaps to believe in the miraculous.

Catholics do not generally ask for miracles. They leave the extraordinary in the hands of God. They are quite conscious that before prayer of petition there must be offered prayer of adoration and thanksgiving as their bounded duty to a Creator and to themselves. Spiritual graces, yes, they ask for these, but when it comes to asking for relief from pain and suffering, it is almost as though they thought, "Why should I refuse what is the common lot of humanity? Why should I ask to be spared when I see the suffering of the family next door?" Suffering borne with courage means to the devout mind a participating in the suffering of Christ and, if bravely endured, can lighten the sufferings of others. It is not a cult of suffering. It is an acceptance of the human condition. ◀◀◀

The Catholic Worker
May 1978

Vitality and Religion

Whatever I had read as a child about the saints had thrilled me. I could see the nobility of giving one's life for the sick, the maimed, the leper. Priests and sisters the world over could be working for the littlest ones of Christ, and my heart stirred at their work. Who could hear of Damien—and Stevenson made the whole world hear of him—without feeling impelled to thank God that he had made man so noble?

But there was another question in my mind. Why was so much done in remedying the evil instead of avoiding it in the first place? There were day nurseries for children, for instance, but why didn't fathers get money enough to take care of their families so that the mothers would not have to go out to work? There were hospitals to take care of the sick and infirm, and, of course, doctors were doing much to prevent sickness, but what of occupational diseases, and the diseases which came from not enough food for the mother and children? What of the disabled workers who received no compensation but only charity for the rest of their lives?

Disabled men, men without arms and legs, blind men, consumptive men, exhausted men with all the manhood drained from them by industrialism; farmers gaunt and harried with debt; mothers weighted down with children at their skirts, in their arms, in their wombs, and the children ailing, rickety, toothless—all this long procession of desperate people called to me. Where were the saints to try to change the social order, not just to minister to the slaves but to do away with slavery?

St. Peter said, "Servants, be subject to your masters with all fear, not only to the good and gentle but also to the forward" (1 Peter 2-18). And the Socialists said, "Workers of the world unite, you have nothing to lose but your chains." Our Lord said, "Blessed are the meek," but I could not be meek at the thought of injustice. I wanted a Lord who would scourge the money lenders out of the temple, and I wanted to help all those who raised their hand against oppression.

Religion, as it was practiced by those I encountered (and the majority were indifferent), had no vitality. It had nothing to do with everyday life; it was a matter of Sunday praying. Christ no longer walked the streets of this world, He was two thousand years dead and new prophets had risen up in His place.

Chapter Four
From Union Square to Rome

9

Peace

THE CALL TO OPPOSE VIOLENCE

We see the worst of the poor, as we see the worst of the rich. We see idleness in a generation which has been brought up in idleness. We see drunkenness and vice in their worst forms. If we dwelt on this dark picture we should lose hope; we would dream of an authoritarian state to bring man out of this Egypt in which he has dwelt so long.

But we cannot lose hope, just as we cannot lose faith in the teaching and examples of Jesus Christ. We know that men are but dust, but we know too that they are little less than the angels. We know them to be capable of high heroism, of sacrifice, of endurance. They respond to this call in wartime. But the call is never made to them to oppose violence *with non-resistance,* a strengthening of the will, an increase in love and faith.

We make this call, and we feel we have a right to make this call by the very circumstances of our lives. We know the sufferings which people are already able to endure; we know their capacity for suffering as the comfortable, those in high places, can never know it. We know it in the response which *The Catholic Worker* has met with throughout the land. We know it in the response of those very poor upon our bread lines who are helping us in carrying on the work all over the country.

To respond in this way is to do away with war. A people thus trained to recognition of spiritual values will overcome the oppressor, the conquered will overcome the conquerors.

A faith which will be crushed by war, will be built up by such a peace. There is no dishonor in such a peace. Men will lay down their lives for their friends, and in losing their lives they will save them. ∽

The Catholic Worker
September 1940

THE MESSAGE OF LOVE

Young men in the draft age feel caught and torn in their humility and in their desire to share the sufferings of others, and in their very real desire to fight the gigantic evils of this world under whatever name they are called. Some of them are having the grace to resist, to oppose the draft, to oppose participation in fruitless slaughter. But if they do it with pride, with condemnation of others, with bitterness, then their stand is questionable also. It is true they will suffer with bitterness, and even the Little Flower herself said that bitterness was a part of suffering that made it harder. If they are jailed there are plenty of opportunities for the works of mercy in jail among the poor there. They will be even more on the side of the poor.

If they obey the call as we have seen quite a number go, against their convictions, let us pray that they have opportunity to minister to the suffering. There is no due deliberation and full consent of the will in wartime, but a blind instinct for self-preservation. We can make no judgments on the armies involved, but on war itself, the means used of atomic warfare, obliteration bombing, the ever-increasing use of destruction to wipe out ideas, philosophies. We can quote Ezekiel who wrote, "Woe to the Shepherds who do not feed their sheep the gospel of peace."

It grows ever harder to talk of love in the face of a scorning world. We have not begun to learn the meaning of love, the strength of it, the joy of it. And I am afraid we are not going to learn it from reading the daily papers or considering the struggles that are taking place on the other side of the world and in the United Nations halls here at home.

We are the little ones, and we can only pray to the saints of our days, the little saints, to disclose to us this hidden world of the gospel, this hidden God, this pearl of great price, this kingdom of heaven within us. It is only then can we learn about love and rejoicing, and it is the meaning of life and its reward.

We talk of one world, and our common humanity, and the brotherhood of man, of principles of justice and freedom which befit the dignity of man, but from whence does he derive this dignity but that he is the son of God?

The one lesson which is reiterated over and over again is that we are one, we pray to be one, we want to love and suffer for each other, so let us pray and do penance in each little way that is offered us through the days, and God will then give us a heart of flesh to take away our heart of stone and with our prayers we can save all those dying each day, knowing that God will wipe away all tears from their eyes.

Lest these words which I write on my knees be scorned, know they are St. John's words, the apostle of love, who lived to see "charity grow cold" and who never ceased to cry out, "My children, love one another."

It is the only word for Christmas when love came down to the mire, to teach us that love.

The Catholic Worker
December 1950

A BETTER WAY

As long as men trust to the use of force—only a superior, a more savage and brutal force will overcome the enemy. We use his own weapons, and we must make sure our own force is more savage, more bestial than his own. As long we are trusting to force—we are praying for a victory by force.

We are neglecting the one means—prayer and the Sacraments, by which whole armies can be overcome. "The King is not saved by a great army," David said. "Proceed as sheep and not wolves," St. John Chrysostom said.

St. Peter drew the sword and our Lord rebuked him. They asked our Lord to prove His Divinity and come down from the cross. But He suffered the "failure" of the cross. His apostles kept asking for a temporal kingdom, even with Christ Himself to guide and enlighten them they did not see the primacy of the spiritual. Only when the Holy Ghost descended on them did they see.

Today the whole world has turned to the use of force.

While we take this stand, we are not condemning those who have seized arms and engaged in war.

Who of us as individuals if he were in Spain today, could tell what he would do. Or in China? From the human natural standpoint men are doing good to defend their faith, their country. But from the standpoint of the Supernatural—there is the "better way"—the way of the saints—the way of love.

Who of those who are combating the Catholic Worker stand would despise the Christian way—the way of Christ? Not one.

Yet again and again it is said that Christianity is not possible—that it cannot be practiced. ∾

The Catholic Worker
September 1938

THE BITTERNESS OF PEACE

It is not just Vietnam, it is South Africa, it is Nigeria, the Congo, Indonesia, all of Latin America. It is not just the pictures of all the women and children who have been burnt alive in Vietnam, or the men who have been tortured, and died. It is not just the headless victims of the war in Colombia. It is not just the words of Cardinal Spellman and Archbishop Hannan. It is the fact that whether we like it or not, we are Americans. It is indeed our country, right or wrong, as the Cardinal said in another context. We are warm and fed and secure (aside from occasional muggings and murders amongst us). We are the nation the most powerful, the most armed and we are supplying arms and money to the rest of the world where we are not ourselves fighting. We are eating while there is famine in the world.

Scripture tells us that the picture of judgment presented to us by Jesus is of Dives sitting and feasting with his friends while Lazarus sat hungry at the gate, the dogs, the scavengers of the East, licking his sores. We are the Dives. Woe to the rich! We are the rich. The works of mercy are the opposite of the works of war, feeding the hungry, sheltering the homeless, nursing the sick, visiting the prisoner. But we are destroying crops, setting fire to entire villages and to the people in them. We are not performing the works of mercy but the works of war. We cannot repeat this enough.

When the apostles wanted to call down fire from heaven on the inhospitable Samaritans, the "enemies" of the Jews, Jesus said to them, "You know not of what Spirit you are." When Peter told our Lord not to accept the way of the cross and His own death, He said, "Get behind me, Satan. For you are not on the side of God but of men." But He also had said, "Thou art Peter and upon this rock I will build my church." Peter denied Jesus three times at that time in history, but after the death on the cross, and the Resurrection and the Descent of the Holy Spirit, Peter faced up to Church and state alike and said, "We must obey God rather than men." Deliver us, O Lord, from the fear of our enemies, which makes cowards of us all. ∝

The Catholic Worker
January 1967

THE WORKS OF WAR

Christ commanded His followers to perform what Christians have come to call the works of mercy: feeding the hungry, giving drink to the thirsty, clothing the naked, sheltering the harborless, visiting the sick and prisoner, and burying the dead. Surely a simple program for direct action, and one enjoined on all of us. Not just for impersonal "poverty programs," government-funded agencies, but help given from the heart at a personal sacrifice. And how opposite a program this is to the works of war which starve people by embargoes, lay waste the land, destroy homes, wipe out populations, mutilate and condemn millions more to confinement in hospitals and prisons.

On another level there is a principle laid down, much in line with common sense and with the original American ideal, that governments should never do what small bodies can accomplish: unions, credit unions, cooperatives, St. Vincent de Paul Societies. Peter Maurin's anarchism was on one level based on this principle of subsidiarity, and on a higher level on that scene at the Last Supper where Christ washed the feet of His Apostles. He came to serve, to show the new Way, the way of the powerless. In the face of Empire, the Way of Love. ∾

The Catholic Worker
May 1972

10

Conversion

A GREAT DISCOVERY

It began out in California where the family had moved from New York a year before. We were living in Berkeley in a furnished house, waiting for our furniture to come around the Horn. It was Sunday afternoon in the attic. I remember the day was very chilly, though there were roses and violets and calla lilies blooming in the garden. My sister and I had been making dolls of the calla lilies, putting rosebuds for heads at the top of the long graceful blossom. Then we made perfume, crushing flowers into a bottle with a little water in it. Even now I can remember the peculiar, delicious, pungent smell.

And then I remember we were in the attic. I was sitting behind a table, pretending I was the teacher, reading aloud from a Bible that I had found. Slowly, as I read, a new personality impressed itself on me. I was being introduced to someone and I knew almost immediately that I was discovering God.

I know that I had just really discovered Him because it excited me tremendously. It was as though life were fuller, richer, more exciting in every way. Here was someone that I had never really known about before and yet felt to be One whom I would never forget, that I would never get away from. The game might grow stale, it might assume new meanings, new aspects, but life would never again be the same. I had made a great discovery. ∾

Chapter Two
From Union Square to Rome

SURPRISED BY PRAYER

Whate I was a child, my sister and I used to keep notebooks in the publishers' dummies we occasionally got hold of. Recording happiness made it last longer, we felt, and recording sorrow dramatized it and took away its bitterness; and often we settled some problem which beset us even while we wrote about it.

Those early diaries had been lost long since, some of them destroyed. But when I moved down to the country and some months later entered into a common law marriage, my peace and happiness were such that I once again took to keeping a notebook.

It was a peace, curiously enough, divided against itself. I was happy but my very happiness made me know that there was a greater happiness to be obtained from life than any I had ever known. I began to read and think and ponder, and I notice from my notebooks that it was at this time that I began to pray more earnestly.

Because I feel that this period of my conversion is so joyous and lovely, I wish to write at length, giving the flavor, the atmosphere, the mood of those days. So I continue from those notebooks that I filled so copiously, especially during the long first winters of the few years I spent in the country:

November

I was thinking the other day of how inadequately we pray. Often in saying the Our Father, I find myself saying by rote the first four lines and throwing my heart into the last, asking for bread and grace and forgiveness. This selfishness humiliates me so that I go back to the beginning again in order to give thanks. "Hallowed be Thy Name. Thy Kingdom come." Often I say no other prayer.

I am surprised that I am beginning to pray daily. I began because I had to. I just found myself praying. I can't get down on my knees, but I can pray while I am walking. If I get down on my knees I think, "Do I really believe? Whom am I praying to?" And a terrible doubt comes over me, and a sense of shame, and I wonder if I am praying because I am lonely, because I am unhappy.

But when I am walking up to the village for the mail, I find myself praying again, holding the rosary in my pocket that Mary Gordon gave me in New Orleans two years ago. Maybe I don't say it right but I keep saying it because it makes me happy.

Then I think suddenly, scornfully, "Here you are in a stupor of content. You are biological. Like a cow. Prayer with you is like the opiate of the people." And over and over again in my mind that phrase is repeated jeeringly, "Religion is the opiate of the people."

"But," I reason with myself, "I am praying because I am happy, not because I am unhappy. I did not turn to God in unhappiness. In grief, in despair, to get consolation, to get something from Him."

And encouraged that I am praying because I want to thank Him, I go on praying. No matter how dull the day, how long the walk seems, if I feel low at the beginning of the walk, the words I have been saying have insinuated themselves into my heart before I have done, so that on the trip back I neither pray nor think but am filled with exultation.

Along the beach I find it appropriate to say the *Te Deum* which I learned in the Episcopalian church. When I am working about the house, I find myself addressing the Blessed Virgin and turning toward her statue.

It is so hard to say how this delight in prayer has been growing on me. Two years ago, I was saying as I planted seeds in the garden, "I must believe in these seeds, that they fall into the earth and grow into flowers and radishes and beans. It is a miracle to me because I do not understand it. Neither do naturalists understand it. The very fact that they use glib technical phrases does not make it any less a miracle, and a miracle we all accept. Then why not accept God's miracles?"

I am going to Mass now regularly on Sunday mornings. ⁌

Chapter Nine, Ten
From Union Square to Rome

THE FINAL OBJECT OF LOVE

"Thou wouldst not seek Him if thou hadst not already found Him," Pascal says, and it is true too that you love God if you want to love Him. One of the disconcerting facts about the spiritual life is that God takes you at your word. Sooner or later one is given a chance to prove his love. The very word "diligo," the Latin word used for "love," means "I prefer." It was all very well to love God in His works, in the beauty of His creation which was crowned for me by the birth of my child. . . . The final object of this love and gratitude was God. No human creature could receive or contain so vast a flood of love and joy as I often felt after the birth of my child. With this came the need to worship, to adore. I had heard many say that they wanted to worship God in their own way and did not need a Church in which to praise Him, nor a body of people with him to associate themselves. But I did not agree to this. My very experience as a radical, my whole makeup, led me to want to associate myself with others, with the masses, in loving and praising God. ∞

Part Two
The Long Loneliness

THE ORDER OF BELONGING

What a driving power joy is! When I was unhappy and repentant in the past I turned to God, but it was my joy at having given birth to a child that made me do something definite. I wanted Tamar to have a way of life and instruction. We all crave order, and in the Book of Job, hell is described as a place where no order is. I felt that "belonging" to a Church would bring that order into her life which I felt my own had lacked. If I could have felt that communism was the answer to my desire for a cause, a motive, a way to walk in, I would have remained as I was. But I felt that only faith in Christ could give the answer. The Sermon on the Mount answered all the questions as to how to love God and one's brother. I knew little about the Sacraments, and yet here I was believing, knowing that without them Tamar would not be a Catholic. ∞

Part Two
The Long Loneliness

New Life in Christ

These pages are hard to write. The struggle was too personal. It was exceedingly difficult. The year passed and it was not until the following winter that the tension reached the breaking point. My health was bad, but a thorough examination at the Cornell clinic showed only nervous strain.

Finally with precipitation, with doubts on my part at my own unseemly haste, I made the resolution to bring an end to my hesitation and be baptized.

It was in December, 1927, a most miserable day, and the trip was long from the city down to Tottenville, Staten Island. All the way on the ferry through the foggy bay I felt grimly that I was being too precipitate. I had no sense of peace, no joy, no conviction even that what I was doing was right. It was just something that I had to do, a task to be gotten through. I doubted myself when I allowed myself to think. I hated myself for being weak and vacillating. A most consuming restlessness was upon me so that I walked around and around the deck of the ferry, almost groaning in anguish of spirit. Perhaps the devil was on the boat.

Sister Aloysia was there waiting for me, to be my godmother. I do not know whether I had any other godparent. Father Hyland, gently, with reserve, with matter-of-factness, heard my confession and baptized me.

I was a Catholic at last though at that moment I never felt less the joy and peace and consolation which I know from my own later experiences religion can bring.

A year later my confirmation was indeed joyful and Pentecost never passes without a renewed sense of happiness and thanksgiving. It was only then that the feeling of uncertainty finally left me, never again to return, praise God! ❧

Chapter Eleven
From Union Square to Rome

11

Trials

FEBRUARY BLUES

"Even if only one person were served and helped by the House of Hospitality, the Catholic Worker would be repaid and could feel that its labors were not in vain," said one of the editors during the month, when a bit of wrangling was going on at the apartment.

It was early in the year, when the February blues had taken possession of everyone. The cold permeated, vitality was low, the winter seemed interminable. There was a fuss because one girl likes plenty of fresh air and another one thought she had enough of it during the day, tramping the streets looking for work and wanted a snug airlessness at

127

night. There was a fuss about whether there should be a sign in the bathroom saying: "Wash out the tub."

The editors, too, felt that their strength was not enough to keep up with the duties of each day. Getting out a paper seemed a simple task compared to the innumerable things which came up every day in regard to the ten girls housed down the street; the feeding of the staff and of the countless visitors who came in; the getting ready for the Catholic Workers' School; the doling out of clothes contributed and solicited by willing friends of the paper and needy neighbors respectively.

Yes, life seemed too complicated just a week or so ago. One day there was one problem after another. Minutes and hours and days were taken up with doing everything else in the world except getting out a paper and answering letters in connection with that paper.

And then—it is the way life goes—all difficulties seemed to resolve themselves. Matters were adjusted and now everything runs smoothly again. ◁∽

Chapter Two
House of Hospitality

CULTIVATING A SPIRIT OF HUMILITY

It has been hard lately. Not only outside criticism but criticism from within, the grumbling, the complaints, the insidious discontent spread around by a few—these trials are hard to bear.

However, the thing is to bear it patiently, to take it lightly, not to let it interfere with the work. The very fact that it is hard shows how weak I am. I should be happy, however, to think that God believes me strong enough to bear these trials, otherwise I would not be having them. Father Lallemant says that we must beware when things are going too smoothly. That is the time when no progress is made.

Oh dear, I am reminded of St. Teresa [of Avila] who said, "The devil sends me so offensive a bad spirit of temper that at times I think I could eat people up."

I'm glad that she felt that way, too. St. Thomas said there is no sin in having a righteous wrath provided there is no undue desire for revenge.

I'm afraid I am very stiff necked. I shall read the Office and go to sleep. But first to concoct a rule for the coming year. (I read in Tanqueray that a rule of life was necessary for all, laymen as well as cleric.)

The Catholic Worker to be in the hands of St. Joseph, and Teresa and I to continue under our novice mistress, the little St. Thérèse, who alone can teach us how to do the little things and cultivate a spirit of humility. St. Joseph is also taking care of me this year.

"Can you not watch one hour with me?"

I shall remember this whenever I am tired and want to omit prayer, the extra prayers I shall set myself. Because after all I am going to try to pray the simplest, humblest way, with no spiritual ambition.

Chapter Seven
House of Hospitality

The Mystery of Suffering

The only answer to this mystery of suffering is this. Every soul seeks happiness either in creatures (where it cannot be satisfied in the long run) or in God.

God made us for Himself.

We must die to the natural to achieve the supernatural, a slow death or a quick one. It is universal. "Unless the grain of wheat fall into the ground and die, itself remaineth alone, but if it die, it beareth much fruit." All must die; it is a universal law very hard for us to realize.

If this mind or this flesh is an obstacle, we will suffer the more when this tremendous Lover tries to tear from us all veils which separate us. Some suffering is more visible, some hidden. If we long for beauty, the more our faith is tried, as though by fire, by ugliness. The more we long for love, the more all human love will be pruned, and the more we will see the venom of hatred about us. It is a pruning, a cutting away of love so that it will grow strong and bear much fruit. The more we long for power, the more we will destroy and tear down until we recognize our own weakness.

But still, suffering is a mystery as well as a penalty which we pay for others as well as for ourselves.

How gigantic was that first Sin, that turning from God! All nature travailleth and groaneth even until now because of it, St. Paul says. The blackness of it, the peculiar hideousness of it, the loathsome perverseness of it, the empty, sterile, grotesque horror of it can scarcely be realized except as we see an echo of it in every sin and crime around us. . . .

The mystery of suffering. I feel presumptuous in writing of so high and lofty a thing. It is because I am not now suffering that I can write, but it is also because I have suffered in the past that I can write.

I write to *comfort* others as I have been comforted. The word comfort too means to be strong together, to have fortitude together. There is the reminder of community. Once when I suffered and sat in church in a misery while waves and billows passed over me, I suddenly thought, with exultation, "I am sharing suffering," and it was immediately lightened. But usually it is as the Little Flower said: "Let us suffer if need be with bitterness and without courage. Jesus truly suffered with sadness. Without sadness, would the soul suffer? And we would suffer generously, grandly; what an illusion!" ❧

October
On Pilgrimage

A Sense of Failure

Tonight Teresa had a nosebleed, a headache and a stomachache, and although the latter probably came from eating green pears, as she confessed, still to think of the little time I have with her, being constantly on the go, having to leave her to the care of others, sending her away to school so that she can lead a regular life and not be subject to the moods and vagaries of the crowd of us! This is probably the cruelest hardship of all. She is happy, she does not feel torn constantly as I do. And then the doubt arises, probably she too feels that I am failing her, just as the crowd in Mott Street and the crowd here feel it.

"You are always away."

And then when I get to Boston—"This is your work, why are you not up here more often?"

Never before have I had such a complete sense of failure, of utter misery.

"O spiritual soul, when thou seest thy desire obscured, thy will . . . constrained, and thy faculties incapable of any interior act, be not grieved at this, but look upon it rather as a great good, for God is delivering thee from thyself, taking the matter out of thy hands. . . . The way of suffering is safer, and also more profitable, than that of rejoicing and of action. In suffering, God gives strength, but in action and in joy the soul does but show its own weakness and imperfections." *St. John of the Cross.*

"Personality is compounded of the body with its appetites and the soul with its rational will; concupiscence springs from original sin and leads to actual sin; it often anticipates reason and is thus a hindrance to the good a man really wants to do: unwished for uprising of temper is a good instance." *St. Thomas.*

Chapter Nine
House of Hospitality

Love in Action

I must recall the words again of St. Teresa—that the only way we can show our love for God is by our love for our fellows. And not an abstract love either. If I cannot remember and contemplate my own worse sins, hidden, and more subtle, then God help me! And if I cannot be patient under trials which the Lord compliments me by sending me, then all my other work is vain. It is not by editing a paper or by writing and speaking that I am going to do penance and achieve sanctity, but by being truly loving and gentle and peaceful in the midst of trouble. Father Lallemant says that when we are comfortable, beware. It is only when things are hard that we are making progress. God is good to send trials. They are a special mark of love.

[Jean-Pierre] de Caussade says that those circumstances which surround us are the very ones God wills for us.

Dear Lord, keep us from pride and self will! Help us to love one another. It is easy to love saints. What do we know about each other's inward struggles.

"Love in action is a harsh and dreadful thing compared with love in dreams." Father Zossima in *The Brothers Karamazov*. ∾

Chapter Seven
House of Hospitality

Community

AN ACT OF COMMUNITY

The reason we write is to communicate ideas, and the reason for getting out *The Catholic Worker* each month is to communicate with our brothers (there are sixty-three thousand subscribers and there may be many more readers). We must overflow in writing about all the things we have been talking and living during the month. Writing is an act of community. It is a letter, it is comforting, consoling, helping, advising on our part, as well as asking it on yours. It is a part of our human association with each other. It is an expression of our love and concern for each other.

"If you have no will for human association, I tell you that you are exposing civilization to the fate of dying in fearful agony," said Pierre Leroux in 1848.

Essentially each one of us is alone, and that makes us first realize our helplessness and then our need of each other and responsibility to each other.

We have been living for fourteen years in a community in Mott street. Every night as we said compline, we said "Visit O Lord this community!" And we meant the street, the neighborhood, the two parishes we lived between, the group where we felt ourselves at home, as once we felt ourselves at home in our families. ❧

The Catholic Worker
October 1950

A LARGE HEADSTRONG FAMILY

One of the reasons we have so many helpers I suppose is that we put up with each other, though criticism is rife, and I sometimes think I am living amongst a bunch of anarchists, so vehemently do all accept Peter Maurin's writings and conversations on personal responsibility and "being what you want the other fellow to be" (and St. Augustine's "Love God and do as you will"). All of which is interpreted as meaning "I am on my own," though living in a community of people. It is thus in a House, and thus on the Farms. Which makes us like large headstrong families of vociferous people. We do keep more or less of a rule on the Farm. We behave like a family in the House in town. People come to meals on time and try to get to bed at a reasonable hour, and it is generally recognized that daily Mass and Communion are fundamental to the work.

"Unless the Lord build the house. . ." We read the *Soul of the Apostolate* and are afraid of the heresy of good works, we try to emphasize the primacy of the spiritual and the necessity of using our spiritual weapons, and in order to get practice in them, we emphasize the retreat and days of recollection. ∾

> *The Catholic Worker*
> January 1948

HOW WE KNOW ONE ANOTHER

From a eulogy for Larry Heaney, a Catholic Worker leader:

We all of us have always been convinced that Sanctity is the only thing in the world worth striving for, the only quality which is of any value whatsoever to God, to us, or to the world. "He has no need of our goods." And when it comes down to it, we haven't so much to give the poor. Except love. And it takes a saint to love, to know what love means, natural love, and supernatural love. Grace builds on nature, they say, and I know you must love naturally, too, to learn what supernatural love is. All this talk of loving people but not liking them is bosh. The Little Flower knew that when she showed such natural affection towards a nun she was tempted to dislike.

When we talked about Larry being a saint, it was no light talk. One doesn't live in community all these years without knowing each other's faults. We are not deceived by one another. We know each other, we know each other "in the breaking of bread," and we have lived intimately together, sharing the same purse, the same house, the same food, the same clothing, to a very great extent. How tremendous this intimacy is. And how we know one another. Our very painful striving for sanctity can get on each other's nerves. Stanley, for instance, used to say, "There are the saints and those who live with the saints, the martyrs." One of his wisecracks, but it meant something. ∞

The Catholic Worker
June 1949

GOD BROUGHT US TOGETHER

Multitudes have passed through our farms and received refreshment and consolation and spiritual light too. And that is not to say that we have not suffered with it all. Criticism, ingratitude, faithlessness, have too often been the reward. Each one seeketh his own. No one can endure on asceticism or on work. There is usually a group who works hard holding things together, doing the palpable visible things; and there is a group too of critics, of talkers; indoctrinators, tearing the Catholic Worker movement apart, but still acknowledging it to be their greatest happiness and joy in life.

God has brought us all together to be instruments of each other's salvation and if ever the old man is to be put to death and the New Man, Jesus Christ, put on ("Put ye on therefore the Lord Jesus Christ") it will be done through community. How we should treasure these sufferings, these criticisms, these wounds to vanity and self-esteem! The way we take them is certainly a measure of our pride and selfishness! We can begin to know ourselves, and so to know Thee, O Lord. (That was a prayer of St. Augustine's.) ∽

The Catholic Worker
May 1953

THE ANSWER TO LONELINESS

Tamar [Day's daughter] is partly responsible for the title of this book [*The Long Loneliness*] in that when I was beginning it she was writing me about how alone a mother of young children always is. I had also just heard from an elderly woman who had lived a long and full life, and she too spoke of her loneliness. I thought again, "The only answer in this life, to the loneliness we are all bound to feel, is community. The living together, working together, sharing together, loving God and loving our brother, and living close to him in community so that we can show our love for Him." ❧

Part Three
The Long Loneliness

THE FINAL WORD IS LOVE

The most significant thing about the Catholic Worker is poverty, some say.

The most significant thing is community, others say. We are not alone any more.

But the final word is love. At times it has been, in the words of Father Zossima [from *The Brothers Karamazov* by Fyodor Dostoyevsky], a harsh and dreadful thing, and our very faith in love has been tried through fire.

We cannot love God unless we love each other, and to love we must know each other. We know Him in the breaking of bread, and we know each other in the breaking of bread, and we are not alone anymore. Heaven is a banquet and life is a banquet, too, even with a crust, where there is companionship.

We have all known the long loneliness and we have learned that the only solution is love and that love comes with community.

It all happened while we sat there talking, and it is still going on. ❧

Postscript
The Long Loneliness

Acknowledgments

The editor and publisher wish to express their gratitude to the creators of The Dorothy Day Library on the Web *at www.catholicworker.org for their permission to use excerpts from Dorothy Day's columns from* The Catholic Worker *newspaper spanning the years 1933 through 1980, and from the following books written by Dorothy Day:*

House of Hospitality, copyright © 1939, Sheed & Ward, New York.

On Pilgrimage, copyright © 1948, Catholic Worker Books, New York.

From Union Square to Rome, copyright © 1938, Preservation of Faith Press, Silver Spring, Maryland.

Other selections came from the following sources:

The Long Loneliness: The Autobiography of Dorothy Day, copyright © 1952 by Harper & Row, Publishers, Inc. Copyright renewed (c) by Tamar Teresa Hennessy. Reprinted by permission of Harper Collins Publishers Inc.

Loaves and Fishes by Dorothy Day, copyright © 1963 by Dorothy Day. Reprinted by permission of Harper-Collins Publishers Inc.

Excerpts of Cardinal John O'Connor's homily appeared on November 13, 1997, in *Catholic New York*, and are reprinted by permission of *Catholic New York*.

For Further Reading

The Long Loneliness: The Autobiography of Dorothy Day. Harper San Francisco, a division of Harper-Collins Publishers, 1997.

Loaves and Fishes by Dorothy Day. Harper & Row, New York, 1963; Orbis Books, Maryknoll, New York, 1997.

Dorothy Day: A Radical Devotion, by Robert Coles. Addison-Wesley Publishing Company, Reading, Massachusetts, 1987.

Love Is the Measure: A Biography of Dorothy Day, by Jim Forest. Paulist Press, New York, 1986; Orbis Books, Maryknoll, New York, 1994.

Praying with Dorothy Day, Companions for the Journey, by James Allaire and Rosemary Broughton. St. Mary's Press, Christian Brothers Publications, Winona, Minnesota, 1995.

Resources From The Word Among Us Press

The Wisdom Series:

Welcoming the New Millennium, Wisdom from Pope John Paul II

My Heart Speaks, Wisdom from Pope John XXIII

Live Jesus! Wisdom from Saints Francis de Sales and Jane de Chantal

Love Songs, Wisdom from St. Bernard of Clairvaux

Walking with the Father, Wisdom from Brother Lawrence

Touching the Risen Christ, Wisdom from The Fathers

These popular books include short biographies of the authors and selections from their writings grouped around themes such as prayer, forgiveness, and mercy.

The New Testament Devotional Commentary Series:

Matthew: A Devotional Commentary

Mark: A Devotional Commentary

Luke: A Devotional Commentary

John: A Devotional Commentary

Acts of the Apostles: A Devotional Commentary

Leo Zanchettin, General Editor

Enjoy praying through the New Testament with commentaries that include each passage of scripture with a faith-filled meditation.

Books on Saints:

A Great Cloud of Witnesses: The Stories of 16 Saints and Christian Heroes by Leo Zanchettin and Patricia Mitchell

I Have Called You by Name: The Stories of 16 Saints and Christian Heroes by Patricia Mitchell

Each book contains inspiring biographies, along with selections of the saints' own writings.

To order call 1-800-775-9673 or order online at www.wau.org